Linda F. Radke's

Promote
Like a Pro

Small Budget, Big Show

Written by
Linda F. Radke
and contributors

Edited by
Salvatore Caputo

Published by
Five Star Publications, Incorporated
Chandler, Arizona

Linda F. Radke's Promote Like a Pro: Small Budget, Big Show
Copyright © 2000 by Linda F. Radke, Chandler, Arizona USA

Published 2000 by Five Star Publications, Incorporated
Chandler, Arizona
Printed in the United States of America

Requests for permissions should be addressed to:
Five Star Publications, Incorporated
P.O. Box 6698
Chandler, AZ 85246-6698
(480) 940-8182 • Fax (480) 940-8787
e-mail: **Radke@FiveStarSupport.com**
websites: **www.BookProducer.com** and
www.CheapPublicity.com

Library of Congress Cataloging-in-Publication Data

Radke, Linda F. 1952–
Linda F. Radke's Promote Like a Pro: Small Budget, Big Show /
written by Linda Radke and contributors; edited by Salvatore Caputo
    p.cm.
    Includes index.
    ISBN: 1877749-36-2
    1. Sales promotion. 2. Self-presentation. I. Title: Promote Like a
    Pro. II. Radke, Linda III. Title

HF5438.5 .R33 2000
658.8'2--dc21

Editor: Salvatore Caputo   **Assistant Editor:** Sue DeFabis
Proofreader: Kevin Dietz   **Indexer:** Michelle B. Graye
Cover design, book design, and production: Kim Scott

Table of Contents

Part I: Linda Radke's Promote Like a Pro: Small Budget, Big Show

Part II: The Inside Scoop

Chapter 1: Publicity and Marketing

About the Author

Photo by Portraits by Reg

Linda Radke, president of Five Star Publications, Incorporated, has parlayed a variety of different opportunities into a successful, award-winning, and continually evolving career.

Radke graduated from Arizona State University in 1976 with a degree in special education and elementary education. Fresh out of school, she worked as an instructor at Arizona State University in a program designed to aid special-ed students into the mainstream of higher education. For two years after she finished that project, she taught sixth grade.

When she realized the truth of the saying "it's hard to find good help," Radke founded her own household employment agency in Scottsdale, Arizona. Then, when she realized that many of the people who wanted to use her firm's services simply couldn't afford them, she compiled her advice into a book, *The Domestic Screening Kit*, which she self-published. Now hooked on books, she wrote and published *Options: A Directory of Child and Senior Services*, and then *Nannies, Maids & More: The Complete Guide for Hiring Household Help*.

Fired up by this success, Radke launched Five Star Publications imprint in 1985. Since then, she has written *The Economical Guide to Self-Publishing: How to Produce and Market Your Book on a Budget* (a 1996 Writer's Digest Book Club Selection), *That Hungarian's in my Kitchen* (a cookbook), and *Household Careers: Nannies, Butlers, Maids & More. Household Careers* received the 1994 AACE Citation for Career Education Initiatives, first place in the 1994 Arizona Press Women's Communications Contest, and honorable mention in the 1994 National Federation of Press Women's Communications Contest.

In her role as publisher, she's helped dozens of authors to produce their books and began Publishers Support Services, a firm devoted exclusively to aiding book writers in their work. Her clients and their books have been covered by: "60 Minutes," FOX News, *Ladies Circle*, *Ladies Home Journal*, the *Wall Street Journal*, *Kiplinger's Personal Finance Magazine*, *Success*, the Associated Press, *US Air magazine*, *Library Journal*, *Publishers Weekly*, *Choice*, *Medical Economics*, *Small Press*, *American Medical News*, *The Denver Post*, *The Arizona Republic*, *Business Opportunities*, *Book Watch*, *Rainbow Electronic Reviews*, *Creative Kids*, *Curriculum Review*, *NEA Today*, *Drama/Theatre Teacher*, *The Book Reader*, *Bloomsbury Review*, the *Midwest Book Review*, *Stein Online*, *C-Span2 Book TV*, the *Howard Stern Show*, *The Dr. Toni Grant Show*, and many, many more.

Radke lives in Chandler, Arizona, with her husband and their two sons.

About the Contributors

WILLIAM D. BUSHNELL is a professional book reviewer with more than 400 reviews published. His reviews have appeared in numerous magazines and newspapers, including *Publishers Weekly*, *Library Journal*, *Independent Publisher*, *Maine Times*, *The Sun* newspapers, *Civil War News*, *World War II*, and the *Maine Sunday Telegram*. He also teaches a class on book reviewing at the University of Southern Maine. He lives on an island off Maine.

SALVATORE CAPUTO is a freelance writer and editor. A 21-year veteran of newspapers, he edits and copy-edits manuscripts for Five Star Publications and contributes to a number of magazines, newspapers and websites. He also co-authored *The Insiders' Guide to Phoenix* (Falcon Publishing) and has contributed to the *MusicHound: The Essential Album Guide* (Visible Ink Press) series. He lives in Tempe, Arizona, with his wife and four kids.

LARRY CARLSON has been a full-time instructor in the Department of Mass Communication at Southwest Texas State University in San Marcos since 1985. He teaches broadcast courses in news writing, management and commercial/promotional writing, as well as introductory classes in advertising and public relations. He is a national member of the Radio Television News Directors Association. An award-winning educator, broadcaster and newspaper writer, Carlson has more than two decades of experience in media work. He began his career as a sportscaster for Austin's KVET/KASE Radio and served as a Texas correspondent for NBC Radio, CBS Radio and Associated Press Radio Network. He later worked as editor of two magazines and was the first Sports Information Director for the University of Texas at San Antonio. Carlson created print ads that have appeared in *Newsweek* and *Sports Illustrated* and wrote marketing copy and feature articles for the *San Antonio Express-News*. Carlson, a San Antonio native, lives in the Alamo City with his wife, Jodie.

Photo by Linda F. Radke

ROBERT COLBERT is a content developer with **AccessArizona.com**, a Web portal site produced in Phoenix, Arizona, and webmaster for POWER92 radio. He graduated from Arizona State University with a Bachelor of Arts degree in Journalism. He has spent more than five years working in various retail companies, handling management and promotional responsibilities.

CHARLENE COSTANZO is living her dream—promoting her book, *The Twelve Gifts of Birth* (which has sold more than 250,000 copies), while touring the country with her husband. She previously was the co-owner of Tisket a Tasket, a gift-basket store in Jamestown, New York.

LARRY FOX is founder and president of fox.content, inc., an Internet marketing service for publishers. He has been in the book business for 30 years, with stints in retail and at Prentice Hall, Ziff-Davis Press, and John Wiley & Sons. Larry has been involved in computers since 1980, when he bought a Sinclair ZX-80. He has advanced degrees in English, creative writing, and anthropology. These days when he is not glued to the screen, he enjoys spending time with his kids, bird watching, and teaching his African Grey Parrot the poems of Gary Snyder. He can be reached at **lrfox@foxcontent.com** or by phone at 301-699-9744.

KERRY LEPAGE, ABC, is the owner of Momentum Marketing. She has spent the past five years as an independent consultant specializing in marketing plans, project management and business development. Before she formed her own company, Kerry's marketing career included eleven years of experience in both public and private sectors for small and large companies, and on both the agency and client side of the marketing relationship. Kerry earned her BA in Communications from ASU and her Masters in Business Administration from the University of Phoenix. She is actively involved with the International Association of Business Communicators (IABC) and the Arizona Production Association, and served on the board of Women in Communications, Inc. (WICI) for eight years. Kerry's work has earned her several awards, including a national Clarion Award from WICI and a Silver Quill from IABC. She has also earned professional accreditation from IABC, a designation given to applicants who pass an extensive exam and portfolio review of their communication-management experience.

A native of Brisbane, Australia, ALF NUCIFORA graduated from the University of Queensland with a Bachelor of Arts degree. He furthered his formal education in the United States, attending the Harvard Business School, where he earned his MBA and graduated with honors. Alf began working for two Fortune 500 companies.

He then made the move to the advertising business and later advanced into agency management. Currently, he serves as principal of a marketing-consulting firm. His column, Shoestring Marketing, is syndicated in more than forty business publications throughout the United States. In addition, he presents more than 100 speeches and seminars a year to Fortune 500 companies, organizations, and associations across the country and abroad. His new book, *The Best of Shoestring Marketing*, is devoted to marketing practice for small- to medium-sized businesses. He can be contacted via e-mail at **alf@nucifora.com**, via his website at **www.nucifora.com**, or by fax at 770-952-7834.

SUZI PROKELL began her career working for one of the top public relations and marketing firms in the country. Within six months, she began handling media relations for international health and fitness guru Susan Powter. Ms. Prokell's publicity skills helped launch "The Susan Powter Show" shown in an unprecedented 200-plus markets nationwide. After launching the show, Ms. Prokell resigned from her position to open Prokell Publicity, Inc. (**www.prokell.com**). Based in the Dallas area, she has conducted more than 100 national media tours, placing clients everywhere from "Today," "CBS This Morning" and "Larry King Live" to *USA Today*, *Entrepreneur*, *The Washington Post* and even the cover of *Time*. Ms. Prokell holds a Bachelor of Science degree in Journalism from Texas A&M University and has written articles for *Today's Dallas Woman*, *Study Breaks*, and *Home Office Computing*. Additionally, Ms. Prokell has appeared in *The Chicago Tribune*, *Forbes*, *The Dallas Morning News*, *Attache*, *Income Opportunities*, *Redbook*, *Parents*, *Woman's Day*, *USA Today*, and on Fox Television.

JOE SABAH is the author and creator of the system *How to Get On Radio Talk Shows All Across America Without Leaving Your Home or Office*, a book, audio seminar, and database of 850 shows that interview guests by telephone. He can be reached at 303-722-7200 or by e-mail at **Jsabah@aol.com**.

CAROL STARR of Starr Gift Baskets has been working in the gift-basket field for ten years. After eight years in print, her book, *The How Tos of Gift Baskets* (published by Green Falls Investment Corporation), continues to be a major resource for people seeking to start their own gift-basket businesses, having sold about 40,000 copies. She is currently at work on another book and on developing new gift items.

JOAN STEWART is a media-relations speaker, trainer and consultant. She publishes *The Publicity Hound*, a bimonthly subscription newsletter featuring tips, tricks and tools for free (or really cheap) publicity. She teaches companies, nonprofit organizations and government agencies about how to use the media to self-promote and position themselves as experts. Stewart has 22 years of experience in the newspaper business as a reporter and editor. Most recently, she was editor of *The Business Journal* in Milwaukee, Wisconsin. For more publicity tips, visit her website at **www.publicityhound.com**. Contact Joan Stewart at **jstewart@publicityhound.com**.

Since 1987, VICKIE SULLIVAN, founder and president of Sullivan Speaker Services Inc., has created six-figure revenue streams for her clients using public/professional speaking as a marketing tool. As an agent and market strategist, Vickie has worked with hundreds of speakers to penetrate a wide variety of markets ranging from church groups to international meetings. Vickie is the author of two audiotape series, "Get Those Bookings" and "Springboard Marketing™." She speaks nationally on using public speaking as a marketing tool and on speaking industry trends. Her work has been featured in *The Arizona Republic* and *Home Office Computing*. More information about the speaking industry and speaking opportunities can be found at **www.sullivanspeaker.com**.

BOBBIE THOMAS is the host and executive producer of "Bobbie Thomas Total Talk," a news and public affairs program on WELE (AM 1380) in Ormond Beach, Florida. She moved to the Daytona area from California in 1991, working on a number of television projects for the American Cancer Society. "Total Talk" has been on the air since 1995 and is now available around the world at **www.totaltalk.net**. Join her there live for questions, feedback and e-mail every weekday morning from 7 a.m. to 9 a.m. Eastern time.

JESS TODTFELD has produced segments for television on topics ranging from news and politics to cooking and hair care. He currently works as an Associate Producer, booking and producing celebrity segments for Fox News Channel in New York.

A Phi Beta Kappa graduate of the University of Michigan, SARAH EDEN WALLACE has worked for 15 years in advertising, book publishing and journalism. After a stint as an editor at a publisher of materials for gifted children, she moved to *Phoenix New Times* for five years and then to *The Arizona Republic*, where she launched and edited that newspaper's Healthy Living section. While editing a section of *Phoenix Magazine* for three years, she also wrote freelance articles on health, travel, and business for a variety of regional and national magazines. A 20-year resident of Phoenix, Arizona, Wallace is currently managing editor of Gentle Path Press.

MARY WESTHEIMER has participated in every facet of publishing. During the past decade, she has shared the keys to effective writing, publishing and marketing with thousands of people, while serving as executive director of the Arizona Authors' Association, internal vice president and a founding member of the Arizona Book Publishing Association, a two-term board member of the Publishers Marketing Association, president of Via Press, a journalism and copywriting instructor, and a workshop and seminar facilitator. A former freelance writer and a contributing editor for *America West Airlines Magazine* for eight years, Mary has more than 350 credits in publications including *Columbia Journalism Review, USA Today* and *Publishers Weekly*. She has written, edited, critiqued, contributed to, or published more than twenty books, including *1001 Ways to Market Your Books* (Open Horizons), *The Lifetime Encyclopedia of Letters* (Prentice-Hall), and *The Writers Encyclopedia* (Writer's Digest). Mary's additional background in bookstore management and sales gives her an invaluable perspective on the publishing industry. In 1994, Mary was appointed president of BookZone, one of the oldest and best-known Internet book sites and the Web's largest publisher community. She can be reached by e-mail at **mary@bookzone.com**, and BookZone's site is at **www.bookzone.com**.

Introduction

So you've chosen to promote your own book (or other project). Perhaps the cost of hiring a marketing and public relations firm is too high for your budget, or perhaps you're a hands-on person at heart and you don't want to let go of your baby. No matter why you've made the choice, you're stuck with the question: "Now what?"

You could either work at promoting your project by trial and error or you could get some expert advice. Since you've picked up *Promote Like a Pro*, you've most likely chosen the latter option. So welcome! You've taken an important first step.

Since 1985, Five Star Publications has helped thousands of individuals and/or publishers with their production and marketing needs. Our clients have appeared on CBS' *60 Minutes*, *C-SPAN Book TV*, *The Howard Stern Show*, and hundreds of other radio and television programs. Their projects have been covered by the *Wall Street Journal*, *Kiplinger's Personal Finance*, *Success* and *Money* magazines, *Library Journal*, *Publishers Weekly*, and *Choice*. In addition, our client's books have been featured as selections by Writer's Digest Book Club, The Jewish Book Club, Doubleday Executive Program Book Club, and Eagle Book Clubs, Inc.

Many of our titles have been selected for distribution by Barnes and Noble, Borders, and Waldenbooks, and one of our cookbooks was selected for distribution by Costco Warehouse (formerly The Price Club). Many of our titles are available online through Amazon.com, barnesandnoble.com, and Borders.com.

Five Star Publications has been in this business for the long haul. We've seen our own ups and downs, as well as the highs and lows of the industry. I wrote *The Economical Guide to Self-Publishing* to help the independent publisher make it through the maze with as few bumps and bruises as possible. However, publishing is just half the job of making a successful book. Statistics show that every year more than 50,000 books are published and more than 7,000 new presses come into existence. With this kind of competition, you just can't expect your book to make it by word of mouth. A well-prepared marketing plan is absolutely essential, and if you haven't been involved in a marketing project before, you need a road map.

Promote Like a Pro is meant to be that road map. Although I write from the perspective of a book publisher, the essentials apply to any project you need to promote, from school plays to new businesses. I hope that you'll let *Promote Like a Pro* make your journey a rewarding one.

—Linda F. Radke, Chandler, Arizona
   February 2000

Part I

Promote Like a Pro

By Linda Radke

The Nuts and Bolts of Publicity

Producing a book is like building a house. You don't want to build a home without blueprints, and you don't want to produce a book without a plan. Like a house, a book cannot succeed without a good foundation. That foundation is the strength of the writer and the information the writer presents. From there, the framework includes the design of the book, the typefaces used, the binding and the cover. When all those elements come together, the house is built—but it's not sold yet.

To sell it, you need to get the word out that you've got a good book that deserves to be read. To get the word out, you need a plan that can help produce the results you want. A careful gardener who fertilizes the soil and plants seeds in organized rows knows where to expect plants to sprout and produces healthier plants than someone who thinks that scattering the seeds and watering the soil is all there is to planting. Although getting publicity is not as predictable as planting, you don't get publicity without planting the right seeds. When you do, you can enjoy the results of your efforts throughout the life of your book, but planting the seeds does not mean the work is over. Just as the gardener must continue to water, weed, and sometimes prune plants, you will need to do the same. Later in this book, you will see how the promotion of *Profits of Death: An Insider Exposes the Death Care Industries* exemplifies this idea.

Remember that publicity is not advertising. Advertising costs you more than publicity, but its advantage is that when you want the advertisement to run, it will run as soon as you've agreed to pay the bill. Publicity is not so predictable. When you start your publicity campaign, you won't know where or when you will get publicity. You will know only whom you will approach to try to get it. However, publicity has significant advantages over advertising because it comes from a source that isn't interested in selling your book. The media you'll approach for publicity consider it their duty to inform their customers about newsworthy products, and your publicity effort will be aimed at getting them to decide that your project is newsworthy (in other words, worthy of the attention of their readers, viewers, or listeners). Their detachment from your goals gives what they say about your project more credibility than your own sales pitches. This is why books proudly print quotations from positive reviews on their covers. Good publicity is worth a great deal and is the most important catalyst to get your marketing efforts moving.

I want to make this trip as pleasant as possible by leading you to the shortcuts and around the pitfalls. During my years in business, I have traveled this road many times. I've experienced the same pitfalls and taken the same shortcuts. You should look to this manual as one looks to a travel agent when planning a vacation—think of *Promote Like a Pro* as your Publicity Agent. This is not going to be an easy trip, but this manual will save you time and money, and will keep you from traveling the wrong roads. With commitment, persistence, and the ability to follow through on each aspect of this manual, you will put yourself in the best position to garner the publicity you seek for your book.

Remember, though, that all you can control is your own efforts. That's another reason that publicity is like planting seeds: you can fertilize the soil, carefully tend the crops, and still a storm can destroy your efforts or a bumper crop can cause oversupply and ruin the market. A farmer doesn't let this fact of life discourage him, and neither should you.

Cost vs. Quality

Book production and marketing are closely related. When we at Five Star Publications are hired to produce a book, we work closely with a client in the selection of the book's title and cover design. It seems we can never have enough sets of eyes proofreading a book. So, if you are working with a limited budget and are tempted to cut costs on the production of your book, be careful. A poorly designed cover will cost you distribution, and the title might cost you marketability. Think what that will ultimately cost you versus paying $700 to $2,000 for a professionally designed cover. After all, it is your baby, and you will be living with the results for a long time to come.

Let's talk about the appearance of your book. Although the old saying "You can't judge a book by its cover" might be true some of the time—trust me, your book will be judged by its cover! It's hard to discuss how you are going to market your book without first discussing whether your book is dressed for success.

Dressed for Success?

Distributors are going to classify your book as A, B, or C. The A books will be offered distribution agreements, the B books in most cases will be turned down with an explanation, and the C books will simply be turned down without explanation. Five Star Publications has been asked to evaluate certain B books for a national distributor. The distributor wants the publishers of these titles to know why they were not selected for distribution and what they could do to improve their chances. Many well-written and edited books were turned down because of their appearance. Ask yourself the following questions to see whether your book has a chance of passing through the channels to distribution. (Although these questions deal with the outward appearance of your book, it should go without saying that your book needs to be well written and properly edited. There's no point in dressing up or trying to sell a bad book.)

1. Does your book have a dynamic cover?
2. Do you have endorsements on the back cover?
3. If you have a foreword written, is the word foreword spelled correctly? (Foreword is the most frequently misspelled word in books we evaluate.) Is the foreword written by a known authority?
4. Does the title tell the reader what your book is about?

5. Is your book bound with an easily read spine?
6. Does your book have a UPC and Bookland EAN bar code?
7. Does the interior of your book have a professional layout and design?

If you answer "No" to just one of the above questions, it's likely a distributor would not consider your book suitable for distribution. All of which points out one of the basic principles of all your marketing efforts: in order to fulfill your needs, you need to fulfill the needs of someone else—whether it's the distributor, the media, or the general public. A "my way or the highway" attitude won't cut it. If you're determined to reach your goals, some flexibility is important. Respect the other person's needs, and the other person will be more likely to respect yours.

How to Find an Economical Publicist

After reading the publicity basics that follow, you may feel the task is too daunting. Or perhaps you'll find that you don't want to handle some particular facet of publicity—maybe you can write a good press release but hate talking on the phone to make follow-up calls, or you want someone to chart out the right media to contact. In these cases, you may want to take an alternate route and hire a publicist—an economical one, of course—to handle all or part of the promotional campaign.

How do you do that?

The temptation may be great to hire a friend to do the work. Friends can sometimes work cheaply and will do so with the best intentions. You should resist that temptation unless your friend is a professional publicist. A friend with the best intentions does not have the experience or track record to make it worth delegating this crucial job to him or her.

Instead, post a job listing through a Journalism or Marketing education department at your local university or community college. You can also contact publicists' associations for leads or take out a help-wanted ad. Keep in mind that you're looking for people who are qualified to do the job. Get a feeling for what they believe they can do and determine whether it matches your goals. (For example, do they want to work full time, while you can only afford a part-time person?) Don't jump at the first person that comes along. Make sure you think this decision through carefully.

Before the Publicity Begins

Distribution is a large part of selling your books. You can promote your book to the far corners of the earth, but if you can't get a distributor to take it on, all your work will have been in vain. What good is it if, thanks to your brilliant publicity efforts, someone hears about your book but can't get hold of it? In a market that expects instant gratification, the book needs to be available when people hear about it. That's why authors on talk shows will mention that their book is available at the major book-selling chains or through an online address such as *amazon.com* or through a toll-free number.

In order to ensure that your book will be in new markets in a timely manner, you need to work with distributors. To establish your distribution channels, start by contacting such national wholesale distributors as Ingram and Baker & Taylor. Remember that they act as wholesalers that warehouse your book and do not have sales representatives who sell to the bookstores. Their only function is to fill orders from the bookstores, and orders are generated by the marketing efforts of the author and/or publisher.

Here's how it works. Imagine that your publicity efforts in a new market cause people to ask about your book at a local bookstore. If you've been exceptionally efficient, the book will be on the shelves already. If not, however, the bookstore buyer will call your distributor and order several copies. No fuss. No muss.

Why couldn't the buyer call you directly to order the book? Think about what's involved with that. If the bookstore buyer has to order books from each separate publisher, the buyer would have to a) keep track of all the publishers, b) write hundreds of small checks to each publisher, and c) if orders didn't show up promptly, the buyer might have to make dozens of calls to different publishers to track down the errant orders. Distributors take away all those hassles, essentially offering one-stop shopping to the bookstore buyers.

Although they reduce risk and hassle for buyers, I learned the hard way that dealing with distributors introduces an element of risk for the publisher.

First, you need to understand the mechanics of working with a distributor. If a distributor agrees to stock your book, you ship to the distributor the agreed-upon number of books at a hefty discount. Currently, the majority of distributors require a 55 percent discount—and some of them will require the publisher to pay for shipping. Although 55 percent may seem unreasonably high to the novice publisher, you have to remember that the distributor also has to offer a discount ranging from 40 percent to 45 percent to the bookstores. So, the distributor's profit comes in the margin between the discount you give the distributor and the discount the distributor gives to the bookstore. National wholesale distributors generally promise to make full payment within 90 days.

Library distributors fulfill the same function for library buyers. With library distributors, such as Quality Books and Unique Books, the books are sold on consignment. In 90 days, these distributors send you a check for what has sold, along with each month's sales report. (When they place their first order with you, they will require 20 to 30 book covers, too. For this and other publicity/marketing purposes, it is important to have the printer run off 100 to 500 extra book covers when you have your book printed.) You can expect library distributors to carry your book from 12 to 18 months, and they will return any unsold books, at their expense, at the end of the agreement. After the agreement ends, they will order single copies from you if there is additional interest. (An important note for self-publishing fiction writers: most library distributors aren't interested in fiction.)

Five Star Publications has worked with numerous distributors, and most of them paid their bills as promised. However, getting paid can be a challenge. One distributor went under with Five Star books in inventory. It was sheer torture trying to get the books back. It might be worth it to write an agreement that lets you get the books back if any form of bankruptcy is declared. Think of it as a "prenuptial" agreement. If the distributor won't agree, it might be a good idea not to "marry" that distributor! This little bit of advice only cost me about $20,000. A major publisher lost more than a million dollars on the same distributor.

Advance Publicity

You can begin your publicity efforts even before the book is published by sending out galleys. Galleys are copies used to proofread the book before the final version is published. Generally speaking, most members of the media want finished books to review. They want to assure their readers that there is a finished book to buy.

However, I encourage you to send galleys to the major trade publications, associations, and the movers and shakers in your field of interest. Reviews from book-industry publications such as *Library Journal*, *Publishers Weekly*, and *Choice* could give you a great endorsement on future mailings, and quotes from them could even be used on the book's back cover if you have a second printing. In addition, their reviews will help generate library sales because these publications are like the Bible to acquisition librarians. Being geared to the book industry, these three publications want to get the word out before the general press. That's why they require galleys and are unlikely to review a book in its finished form. (Every rule has an exception though. For instance, I notified a reviewer at *Library Journal* that *Nannies, Maids & More: The Complete Guide for Hiring Household Help* had been published and that review copies were available. The reviewer requested a copy and wrote it up even though there was no chance to beat the general press to a review.)

I usually wait until I have finished books in hand before starting my campaign to the general-interest media. Since you're working on a budget, you'll most likely want to do as I do to save money. I create an A list of prospective reviewers that will receive a copy of the book for review and the media kit that goes with it. (A description of what goes into a media kit follows later in this section.) Who makes the A list? It's a combination of the media outlets that would be most important to our marketing efforts and the reviewers who would be most likely to give the book a positive review.

Prospective reviewers on my B list get a "media postcard," which tells them a little about the book and asks them to respond if they would like a review copy. The B list should cover reviewers at smaller-circulation publications, those who only marginally reach the market you're seeking, or those who would be less likely to review the book. We would like to put some of the B list prospects on the A list, but economics don't allow us to do so. Creating the B list cuts the considerable cost of mailing books to every prospect, but at the same time keeps the door open to them. Remember, we'd like reviews from all these outlets!

The publicity materials, also known as a press kit or media kit, that you send out with galleys or a finished book will be your first contact with the media. So they, like your book, should be "dressed for success." Remember to take as much care writing and editing these materials as you took with the book. Print materials on personal or business letterhead or on stationery designed especially for the project. Go for businesslike quality here. Poorly printed materials will leave a bad impression. Handwritten notes, although personal, will not appear businesslike. However, it's not objectionable to include a handwritten note that points out some important aspect, such as "author is local," to a prospective reviewer. Keep these notes concise.

When you send out the book or galleys for review, the media kit materials may include:

- A cover letter explaining that you're sending the book for review. For media reviews, do your homework. Find out beforehand who at the newspaper, magazine, or broadcast outlet is the person in charge of book reviews. For copies sent out to experts for their endorsement, explain to them why you chose to send the book (usually because they are experts in the field the particular book covers), and ask them politely for comments that you may quote. In an age of litigation, you might even want to create some form of release that gives you their express permission to use their quotes for the marketing of the book. If you can afford the time, it's always good to call beforehand to gauge the expert's interest.

- A press release. This is a short item, usually about one page in length, announcing that this book will be published on a specific date (or in the case of completed books, it simply announces the book is available) and summarizing the important and notable elements of the book. It's good to mention the author's expertise with the subject matter here.

- A single-page biography of the author.

- A sample of the cover art (as noted above, you should have about 100 to 500 extra book covers printed for publicity purposes at the time your book is printed) and a photograph of the author.

- If you plan to publish more books, you may want to include a brochure or other materials that you use to market your publishing company.

- Many companies put all these materials into a folder of some kind. Folders can be as simple as those bought in an office-supply store or they can have the logo of the publishing company on them or they can be more elaborate. Since you're working on a budget, it's important to remember that the folder is mostly a courtesy to recipients to help them keep your press kit neatly organized. So if you use a folder, buy with that simple function in mind. Go with a solid color that stands out—such as red or black—and use a folder that allows you to insert a business card over one of the pockets. Remember, what goes into the folder is much more important than the folder itself.

As for the B list prospects, my media postcards are professionally written and designed, and you would do well to take care to have them printed professionally. It's important to put your best face on since this will be your B list media's first contact with you. The postcard needs to make the reviewer want to request your book, so it's good to include a representation of the cover and a brief but compelling description of the book, AND, of course, a line or two telling them how to contact you to receive their review copy.

Once you've received some publicity—feature stories or reviews—it's always a good idea to include photocopies of the news clippings. This shows your new publicity prospects that other media outlets have considered your project newsworthy. Bookstores and distributors will be interested in this fact, too.

Get an Early Start

One important thing to remember is that all media work in advance. There is a gap between the last moment when they can accept a request for coverage and the time that such coverage is broadcast or published. The gap is called "lead time." Although major news stories can have a lead time as short as a few minutes on TV or radio and as short as a few hours at newspapers, stories surrounding your book usually will not be on that type of fast track. If you want a story to appear at the time your book is published, you will need to begin making publicity contacts well in advance. So as soon as you know which media you want to target, you need to contact them to find out their lead-time requirements. For instance, magazines generally work three months ahead of time, but a television station won't look at its folder of dated press releases until a few days beforehand. Sunday newspaper sections may work a few weeks in advance, while other sections of the paper might need anywhere from a week to a couple of days' notice to honor a publicity request.

Don't overlook the wire services when determining which media outlets to approach. Wire services, such as the Associated Press, supply newspapers and radio stations with a good deal of news each day. To attract a wire service, your publicity material should emphasize your story's universal nature, so that it will appear newsworthy to the many outlets that subscribe to the service. If the wire service runs a story, it can quickly appear in hundreds of newspapers.

You may also want to explore such services as PR Newswire and Business Wire. These services will send out your press releases to a wide range of media outlets for a fee. The fees might be prohibitive if you go for the whole shooting match, but sales representatives of these services will work with you to get the most bang for your buck and your book. They can target by type of outlet (print or broadcast), by subject area (entertainment, business, sports, etc.), and by geography (national, regional, state, or international), so there is a great deal of flexibility. You'll be assured of getting the word out to multiple outlets, and cut right to the follow-up stage. Both services have branch offices in cities across the country. To find out more, check out their websites at **www.prnewswire.com** and **www.businesswire.com**.

When writing your publicity materials, it's important to keep in mind that you will be competing with many other newsworthy events that are vying for newspaper space and broadcast air time. You can't just tell the media your book is coming out; you must emphasize why it's important for them to cover this book in a timely fashion.

When is the best time to start publicity? Yesterday.

Let me share an example from several years ago. In early summer, I met with my client, Dr. Nelson Haggerson, who had written a biography, and the subject of his biography, Dr. Arlena Seneca. She is a prominent African-American educator who has made major contributions to the education system. The three of us worked together closely on marketing and promoting the book. They told me that the book would be out that August and that they were anxious to have us start their publicity campaign.

I told them that I would be happy to start their campaign in June by creating their media kit and then releasing the information in August, or that they could wait a few months and have their campaign begin in November/December to introduce their book during National Black History Month. National Black History Month lands in February, but most magazines work three months ahead of schedule. So, we let the magazines know about this title in November. When the book hit the stands in February, the campaign was a success. There were several feature stories honoring Dr. Seneca and a local TV station acknowledged her contributions in a 15- to 30-second segment that ran daily to honor prominent African-Americans during National Black History Month.

Publicity Tie-ins

When there is a natural tie-in to something newsworthy like Black History Month, consider it a tide that will help float your boat. The media will be scrambling for news stories in areas like this and will be more receptive to your project. But don't try to force the fit with the tie-in. If you have to do too much explaining to make the connection, the connection will not be credible, and the editor or producer won't buy it.

Publicity tie-ins don't necessarily have to be serious. Let me tell you about the tie-in (pardon the pun) we created for *Tying the Knot—The Sharp Dresser's Guide to Ties and Handkerchiefs*. This was a charming book produced by Andrew Cochran, and Five Star Publications was hired to redo it. We evaluated the cover and found it to be outdated, so we changed the title, gave the book a new cover design, added information about the history of the tie industry, and increased the price of the book from $2.95 to $5.95. (Most of us are in this game to make money, and raising the price gave us more room for working with distributor discounts.) An idea we gave Mr. Cochran is a contest in which participants will be asked to submit the ugliest tie ever received for Father's Day. Who will judge this contest? Who else? Andrew G. Cochran, author of *Tying The Knot*. Any mentions of the contest will automatically publicize his book.

However, you don't have to create events to have an event tie-in (remember the example of the book on Dr. Seneca). Look at your local newspaper's calendar of events. Is there a natural tie-in between your book and some upcoming event? Issue a press release to your local media outlets about it. You can also find books and almanacs that list the various official months (such as Black History Month) and create tie-ins that have national appeal.

It's also a good idea to watch current events. If something happens that ties in with a subject in your book, jump in and point out the connection. It's a good opportunity for authors to write a letter to the editor regarding their stand on current events, and, of course, you'll remember to mention that you're the author of a book that shows your expertise on the subject.

The Challenge of Publicity

There are many decisions to be made in pursuit of publicity, but after years of building publicity campaigns, I've found that the biggest challenge always is: what angle do we use?

Generally speaking, an angle is what makes the particular story interesting and unusual. If something is sufficiently unusual, it will be newsworthy. Remember, if a dog bites a man, that's not unusual, but if a man bites a dog—you've got a news story!

Keep in mind that you are trying to get people who've heard it all to give your book the time of day, so you've got to give them something that will pique their interest.

That means looking at your project from different angles. What makes this book different from all others? What's the most important thing about the book? To whom does it appeal? Is the subject of the book a peculiar passion of the author's? How does this book challenge the conventional wisdom on this subject? These are just some of the questions you can ask yourself to help develop an angle that will get the media interested in devoting precious space or air time to your project.

One angle that's almost a no-brainer is the hometown connection. This is an especially good one for newspapers, radio, and TV in small markets. Do a special news release in the author's hometown to emphasize the author's roots there. If the author no longer lives there, you may also be able to garner some more publicity by gearing a similar release to the town where the author currently lives. Most of these outlets have a strong interest in this angle.

Some books, like *Profits of Death: An Insider Exposes the Death Care Industries*, write their own angles because they deal with controversial, newsworthy subjects. The angle that made the biography of Dr. Seneca newsworthy was its relationship to Black History Month.

If your book is mentioned by a major publication or program, that's another angle to write a press release about. When I was interviewed by *Entrepreneur* magazine, we wrote a news release about it, and the story received attention in our local publications. When Darryl Roberts was featured on *60 Minutes,* we issued a news release about it.

Some books offer tougher challenges. Take Mr. Lloyd Pedersen and his first novel, *The Vintage*. Mr. Pedersen realized after his first book was published—all 885 pages of it!—that he needed publicity. The first agency he hired was unable to get him any. I assumed that they had given it their best shot, as it is extremely difficult to get publicity for unknown authors of fiction. I told him we would need a new angle, and inquired about his age. When he informed me that he was 90 years old, I told him "That's it! That's the angle we need!" We then portrayed him as a first-time author at the age of 90. (He insisted we inform the media that he didn't start the book at the age of 90, but rather at the age of 80!)

As a result of working that angle, several publications and a wire service expressed interest in the story. In fact, the wire service's interest led to a call for a possible interview with Mr. Pedersen from a major late-night talk show. Who could ask for more than that? So sometimes the angle can be the author, rather than the book itself.

You should note one other important factor, although the fact that a book is new isn't considered a newsworthy angle, the book's age will affect your publicity efforts. A book is most likely to be considered newsworthy in its first year. Think of it like a newborn baby—in the first year, everyone wants to take a look, and interest generally wanes after that. Unless there's a sudden groundswell of sales after the first year, hardly any other angle will revive the media's interest in the book.

Marketing Unknown Writers

If there is one thing that will sell books and guarantee publicity for them, it's having an author who is a known quantity—either a public figure or celebrity, like Cher or Howard Stern, or a novelist like Tom Clancy or Stephen King, whose keyboards seem to have the Midas touch. That's why my company, and many other publishers, put so much emphasis on having a foreword written by a well-known individual and then including their name on the front cover. It helps get the public to pay attention.

Of course, the chances are pretty good that you don't have a Cher or Tom Clancy to publicize, so you're faced with the same challenges other publicists face with unknown authors.

Before the book is completed, you should look at it to determine whether there is someone well known in that field who could write a foreword, and approach that person for one. If there are no time constraints, it's best to send a polite business letter asking whether he or she would be interested in reading the book and writing a foreword. If you're pressed for time, phone or e-mail contact may be preferable.

Sometimes, the person to write the foreword will emerge from another aspect of your publicity effort—the search for endorsements. Does the book address a subject area of interest to professional societies, academics, hobby groups, companies, or other easily identifiable groups or individuals? You will want to create lists of potential endorsers similar to those you create for reviewers. Their responses can be incorporated into your publicity materials. We use endorsements when we can in press releases, book fliers, and media postcards.

An unknown's biggest asset for obtaining publicity is credibility: Does the author have credentials? Is the book professionally written, edited, designed, and produced? Positive answers to these questions mean you'll have a credible product. In addition, you'll want to ask these questions: Does the author have the ability to speak before the media? Will the author have a flexible schedule or just want to be interviewed at his or her convenience? Is the book available through local and/or national bookstore chains?

A self-promoter's biggest assets are patience and persistence. When Five Star Publications works for another client, we have to ask ourselves, "Will the author let the publicists complete the job as outlined?" One client canceled his agreement two weeks into the job when he felt he was not gaining his "15 minutes of fame" fast enough. So you have to remember that publicity efforts earn their rewards slowly.

Keep Your Expectations Realistic

I always strive to outline realistic expectations to a client, and I do so at the cost of losing business. I make it a point to explain what publicity can and cannot do for a product or client, and it's important that you know these things, too:

1. Publicity can give you greater visibility.
2. Publicity can lend credibility to you as an expert in your field. Understand that writing a book does not make you an instant

expert. It's having the credentials and the experience that makes you the expert.

3. Publicity keeps distributors and booksellers happier and more likely to keep your book on their shelves. Did you know that if your book makes it into the national bookstore chains and the book doesn't sell within the first 90 days, they will quickly remove it? Why? Because there are 49,999 other titles that are fighting for that same space.

4. Publicity will not guarantee book sales. Clients often ask, "Shouldn't I sell a lot of books if a publication with a circulation of a million or more gives my book a mention?" Statistically, clients feel they should get at least a one percent response. Wrong—that will rarely happen. I have read that a person needs to read about a product 14 times before they will buy it. That's why a continuing publicity effort is necessary. How-to books and cookbooks have the best chance of seeing a few extra sales tied to a radio interview, newspaper review, or any other media mention. Customers like to know what your book will do for them, and if it helps them make money, save money, lose weight, or look younger, you probably have a greater chance of selling books.

We're talking about very small increases of sales from any single mention, but is all the effort to get these few sales worth it? When we were marketing *Kosher Kettle: International Adventures in Jewish Cooking* by Sybil Ruth Kaplan, our efforts landed the book a four-page magazine spread in *Phoenix Home and Garden* along with a mention on the magazine's cover. The magazine hired a designer to set the table, someone to prepare the meals, and a photographer to shoot it all. The cost of that alone would have busted our limited marketing budget, let alone the cost of buying four pages of full-color advertising in any magazine.

Publicity efforts keep your book in front of the public, and when a publication shows interest in your book—especially with something as lavish as the *Kosher Kettle* spread—it lends your book credibility. People appreciate that an objective source thinks your book is worth that type of interest.

As I said before, publicity also keeps your distributors happy. Why do they want to distribute a book that isn't being marketed by the publisher?

When Darryl Roberts, author of the book *Profits of Death: An Insider Exposes the Death Care Industries,* appeared on *60 Minutes* as an expert on the funeral industry, sales of his book shot up. The producer contacted us after reading about him in previous publicity that we had generated, and the two met during a signing that we had arranged at BookExpo, an industry gathering in Chicago. Their crew filmed us during that signing, and the face-to-face interview with Leslie Stahl took place back at his hotel. Eight months later, the segment aired.

What was that interview worth in advertising dollars? Millions. Did it cause him to sell thousands, if not millions, of copies of his book? No—but it did help to establish him as a leading expert in his field. Since then, opportunities as an expert witness have opened up for Mr. Roberts. It is as an expert witness that he will most likely recoup his publishing expenses.

Success Means More Work

OK, you've followed my tips and now a publication or broadcast station is going to publicize your book. Success, right? Sure it is, but that doesn't mean your job is over.

As soon as you know when the review or feature is going to run in a market, you should contact the local bookstores. They can do a number of things to support the publicity you've garnered. The most important, of course, is to have copies of the book on hand and prominently displayed when the review runs.

If a newspaper is going to review the book, you have an excellent opportunity to contact radio and TV in the same vicinity and offer your time as a guest on their station.

Book Signings

Bookstore signings are another possible tool in the publicity kit, although I'm not a big fan of them. The fate of unknown authors at book signings reminds me of an episode of the old sitcom *Newhart*. In this episode, Bob Newhart's character, who was an author of home-remodeling how-to books, was given a book signing at a hardware store. No one came, and no one there even understood why he was there. Let's face it, the known author will have a following and, in most cases, an unknown will not.

However, if you want to brave an author signing, establish yourself with the larger bookstore chains. Go where you can find a crowd of book buyers. Locally, I encourage authors to establish signings with Barnes and Noble. Barnes and Noble (given ample lead time) will issue a nicely produced poster at its expense and possibly feature your signing in its newsletter. The newsletter is distributed in its local stores and sent to those on the chain's private mailing list.

If you stage a book signing, it can't hurt to let the media know. The marketing person at each bookstore will most likely send a news release to the calendar editors of local publications and stations. However, you shouldn't count on them to do your publicity for you. Ask the marketing person to give you a copy of the store's media contact list, issue a press release about the event and send it out. If you like, you can follow up with phone calls to see whether there's any interest in sending a photographer or reporter (or both!) to the event.

Using the World Wide Web

You'll want to use every tool possible for your publicity. The World Wide Web's potential audience is huge, so a website may be an economical way to expose your project to people around the world. (If you have an advertising budget, you may also want to consider advertising on the Web. Because of the interactive nature of Web advertising, in which the ad often leads the potential customer right to an order form, it's easy to track whether the money invested in Web advertising is paying off.)

Should you create your own website? Is it worth the money you would invest in that site to market and promote just one book? Only you can decide.

You can cut some of the investment if you know how to design a Web page yourself. The popular book *HTML for Dummies* can help you there, and Web "publishing" software can help even a novice build decent-looking pages quickly. Remember, though, that you'll get your best, most-winning design from a professional designer.

The other cost involved is in paying for a site to keep the information online. You cannot use a personal home page on such online services as America Online or CompuServe to sell products. If you get significant traffic to such pages, they'll check into it and ask you to move to their more expensive commercial pages. The best thing to do is to shop around for price, but make sure of the service's reliability before making a deal.

What information should be on your website if you choose to do one? Allow me to give another example of a service we provided for Darryl Roberts. When he decided that a website was the correct route for him to take, we created **www.profitsofdeath.com**. His site features a monthly newsletter and can take online orders for his book, which is also advertised in our online bookstore.

If you decide to create a website, it's important to establish it before you send out your publicity, that way you can provide a convenient Web address for the media and public to obtain additional information. Will you sell a lot of books through the Internet? Probably not; however, it will provide you with additional exposure, an increase in bookstore orders, and potentially surprising results.

Take, for instance, this story about Sally Starbuck Stamp and L.A. Kowal, the authors of *The Proper Pig's Guide to Mealtime Manners*. They were asked to be featured guest speakers at a conference on manners aimed at engineering students at a Michigan university. The conference coordinators searched for the word "manners" on the Internet, which brought them to *The Proper Pig's Guide* in our online bookstore, and there they found out about Stamp and Kowal. Who could have imagined beforehand that they would make this type of connection?

If you do choose to create your own website, an easy way to attract people to your site is to offer an online bookstore contest or some other promotional idea. This has proved quite successful for us: "Visit our site and register to win a free book." It's as easy as that.

You can also take advantage of our own **www.CheapPublicity. com** (and services like it) to post information about yourself, your books, and your projects on line. These services make you more accessible to media inquiries and requests for speakers and, thus, are an indirect, but useful, way to get your message out.

Developing Mailing Lists

Mailing lists will be key to your efforts to promote your book. Ideally, when you put them together, they will be in a database program that allows you to print directly onto adhesive labels that can be easily applied to media postcards, envelopes, etc. What programs should you use? We use Act! and Microsoft Access. They offer a great opportunity to store and retrieve any database. Whatever program you use, make sure to keep dated copies of your mailing lists for future use or reference.

Here is some advice from Mary Hawkins, a member of the Five Star family since 1989 and who has recently retired. She not only edited a number of our books, but assisted in the development of many of our mailing lists:

"If someone suddenly says to you (or you realize on your own), 'We need a mailing list for this publication,' where do you start?

"First, you need to ask yourself, 'What is the purpose of my mailing list?' You might need to develop different lists for sending out galleys, news releases, and review copies, or for any other purpose that might crop up.

"Then, you need to know what markets you're trying to reach. 'What print, radio, TV, and computer outlets reach those markets?'

"Also ask yourself, 'What is the subject area?' For instance, it could be cosmetics, sports, cookery, construction, etc."

Hawkins offers this list of her favorite print references (as opposed to online information) for the job of putting together mailing lists:

1. *R.R. Bowker's Literary Market Place* (updated annually, published by R.R. Bowker). To order, write R.R. Bowker, P.O. Box 1001, Summit, NJ 07902-1001, or call (800) 521-8110.

2. *Gale Directory of Publications and Broadcast Media* (updated annually, published by Gale Research). To order, write Gale Group, P.O. Box 9187, APO, Farmington Hills, MI 48333-9187, or call (800) 877-4253.

3. *Encyclopedia of Associations* (Gale Research). To order, write or call Gale Group as noted above.

4. Your phone book, and any other local listings.

In addition to Mary's recommendations, I can tell you that bookstores themselves are another potential source for creating a media contact list within a given market. The marketing person at each bookstore will most likely send a news release to the calendar editors of the local publications and broadcasters. As I mentioned when talking about book signings, don't count on them to do your publicity, but do consider asking for a copy of their media list.

For national publicity, I can also recommend the Bradley directory and Bacon's directory of media outlets. Bacon's can also be purchased on compact disc for your computer. Local libraries often carry these or other similar directories of media outlets, so budget-conscious self-promoters will want to check with their reference librarian, as well.

You can also find publicity leads on the Internet by using search engines. Here are the Internet addresses of several of the top search engines:

- http://www.webcrawler.com
- http://www.yahoo.com
- http://www.excite.com
- http://www.hotbot.com
- http://www.dogpile.com

You'll find that each of these turns up different sources of information, so it's often good to do searches on each of these to maximize the number of leads you turn up.

There are also programs that you can download for free that combine multiple search engines into one big search. Here are the names of two programs that we have used:

- webferret
- Express by Infoseek

Part II

The Inside Scoop

That *Mad* magazine sage, Alfred E. Newman, once said, "Learn from the mistakes of others. You'll never live long enough to make them all yourself." It's funny, but it's also true. I wouldn't have been able to build my business if the only way I learned was through trial and error. I have always sought the wisdom of people who know more about a particular aspect of what I do to help me or teach me.

That's why I asked a group of experts to chime in with their insider perspectives on publicity and marketing. A professional publicist outlines the essentials of a publicity campaign. The print and broadcast media people have offered chapters on how to pitch them successfully. The Internet experts tell us how to use the Internet more effectively. An expert in public speaking explains how to use that forum to successfully promote your products. Marketing experts instruct us on how to build a good marketing plan. We've also included advice from successful self-promoters, who explain how they promoted like pros.

They expand on what I've written in my chapters, clarifying some of the detail work you'll need to cover. As a self-promoter, you need to look at your project from every angle, and these multiple points of view should help you as you plan your campaign.

You will find that the experts echo one another and me when it comes to the basics. Excuse the redundancy, but the repetition should help drive home the real essentials that have worked for a broad spectrum of promoters.

We also may disagree with one another on some specifics or even in our philosophical approach to promotion. This is to be expected. We are all different and bring different tools and strengths to our efforts. For instance, do you hate getting on the phone to call people? Then, you may have to hire someone to do that for you, or you'll have to work harder on mail and e-mail to get results.

The point is that all the experts here are offering advice based on what works for them, and what works for them differs according to their own temperaments and talents.

In any case, whether the experts and I agree or disagree on a specific point, you will need to adapt advice to fit your own situation and make it work for you.

chapter **1**

Publicity
and Marketing

There is a fine line between marketing and publicity, but keep in mind that they are two different things. They should work hand in hand. Marketing considerations include such things as the price of your product, and its title or name, and how to distribute it. Marketing should begin long before the book or product reaches the hands of the public. Publicity is the process of letting people know that you're marketing something. Publicist Suzi Prokell lists the practical steps you can take to publicize your project.

How to Publicize Your Book

By Suzi Prokell

Now that you have your book published, how can you make sure it sells? Publicity is a crucial element for success. Without it, the public has no way of knowing about your work, and the book will simply sit on bookstore shelves with all the others. Publicity is a tool to reel in readers and convince them to buy your book.

A huge misconception about publicity campaigns is their timing. Most authors wait until they have their books completed and printed before thinking about publicity. Unfortunately, by this time, it's too late. Because of production schedules, magazines have a lead time of three to six months. This means that editors need to know of your book three to six months before it is available in bookstores. Editors like to provide their readers with timely information and most will only run book reviews the same month a book is released. After that, the book is considered old news.

The First Step

The first step to a publicity campaign is to determine your target audience. Who is most likely to be interested in your book's subject matter? Once you answer this question, you can begin to research and compile media lists. Media lists should include every print and broadcast media outlet you feel might be interested in reviewing your book, as well as all local media contacts in your hometown. Working the hometown media is a great way to jump-start publicity for your book and determine what pitch sells your book to an editor before approaching national media.

Media lists should include as many different editors at each appropriate media outlet as possible. For example, if you have a book on nutrition, you might contact the book review editor as well as the health, food, and lifestyles editors. This increases your odds of getting coverage in that outlet. A great resource for media lists is the *Bacon's Media Directory*. This is a four-book directory that includes every radio show, television show, magazine, and newspaper in the U.S. and Canada. It's also available on CD-ROM so you can compile your own lists and print labels. However, it's expensive and may not be something you wish to purchase if you have just one book to promote. In this case, you might want to purchase specific media lists from Bacon's by calling 1-800-621-0561.

Once you have a media list, you need to write a news release about your book. Generally, this should be no longer than two pages and include a brief overview as well as anything interesting about the book's subject matter or author. You should also include the book's ISBN number, price, release date, and number of pages. The press release should include a contact name and phone number at the top and should be double-spaced. It's very important to include the vital information in the first paragraph—including the book's title and release date—as most editors make a decision on their interest after reading the first two paragraphs. Most do not read a press release in its entirety so it's important to grab their attention in the first few sentences.

You can hire a writer to draft a press release for you or you can attempt to write one on your own. Your press release needs to be well-written as it is the first, and most times only, impression you give to editors. It is your only tool to generate book reviews.

Now What?

Next, you need to distribute the press release to the contacts on your media list. It is best to send the press release by mail with a color copy of the cover of your book (to give editors something to visualize what they are considering). You should distribute materials to the "long-lead" media first. This includes national magazines and any national television talk shows. Next, you can distribute materials to any radio shows, newspaper book review editors, and your hometown media.

It is crucial to follow up with every person who receives your press release. With this in mind, you may want to plan your press-release distribution effort in phases, or "legs". This will make it easier for you to effectively manage follow-up calls. It's not enough to send the release and assume editors will call if interested. Many times, editors have moved or did not receive your press release, or they may be interested but may not have found the time to call and request a review copy. Which brings us to another tip: be sure to print 25 to 50 galley copies of your book. Have them ready to send upon request. Editors work with tight deadlines and if they express interest, you need to be ready to provide all necessary information immediately or you will lose their interest.

It's also wise to send review copies with the "key" media on your list. Programs such as *Good Morning America* or (if your book is for women) publications such as *Ladies' Home Journal* should receive the press release and a galley at least 90 days before the book's publication. With prominent national media, it's wise to send as much as you can up front to get the best consideration.

Always keep in mind that editors look for news. A new book is not news enough. You must have a timely hook. If a media outlet recently covered your book's subject matter, you might send your book as a response in an attempt to get them to write another story. Another tip: tie your book's subject matter in with current news. For example, during the Bill Clinton-Monica Lewinsky scandal, a book about infidelity would have been timely, thus increasing its odds of attracting publicity.

Book Tours

With the above suggestions, most authors can conduct publicity by phone. Magazine, newspaper, and radio interviews can be done by phone and national television appearances, once booked, are usually paid for by the show. If you have the funds, it is recommended that you conduct a book tour.

A book tour typically consists of two to ten cities that you choose to tour to conduct media interviews. Once you have a city in mind, you develop a media list for that market and distribute materials about four weeks in advance of your trip. If you would like to speak or do a book signing at a local bookstore, you should make arrangements about eight to twelve weeks in advance as calendars fill up quickly.

Book tours are an excellent way for your book to generate and build publicity at local levels, thus creating a buzz about the author and the book. Most authors travel to a different city every week. How do you choose which cities to tour? You can probably determine which markets may be receptive to your book's subject matter. For example, San Francisco is known as "new age," while Houston is conservative. Generally, unless you are an established, well-known author, steer clear of large markets such as New York, Los Angeles, and Chicago. You will likely want to tour smaller markets to maximize your publicity opportunity.

You can conduct a city-by-city book tour at the same time as you conduct a national publicity campaign. The two will feed each other and maximize your coverage. Additionally, as you generate press clippings, you can use those to obtain further coverage. One press clipping can establish much needed credibility with an editor.

Should I Hire a Publicist?

Publicity is a full-time job. It takes persistence and lots of time to reach editors and convince them that they should review your book. Because of this, you might consider hiring an independent book publicist to direct your campaign. Although it can be expensive, it's worthwhile. Book publicists have established relationships with the media and know how to work a pitch. Additionally, it establishes much credibility for an author to have a publicist representing them rather than an author representing him/herself. Having a publicist represent your book will maximize its publicity potential. Publicists know the industry and can tell you up front what needs to be done.

Publicists work with authors to launch and direct complete campaigns and/or to carry on publicity efforts after publishers have stopped theirs. It all depends on your budget. Most publicists work on a monthly retainer basis in which you receive a specified number of hours of service for a flat monthly fee. Fees vary and depend on the complexity of the project.

Remember, publicity is equally as important as publishing your book. The two go hand in hand and without one, the other will fail. As more and more new authors emerge, the industry is realizing the value of publicity. The book business is competitive, just as any other business, but with proper knowledge and planning, you can make your book a success.

Kerry LePage, owner of Momentum Marketing, takes a comprehensive look at the relationship of marketing, advertising, and public relations. She lets the small-budget promoter see how the Big Boys and Girls take on these challenges. It's up to us to adapt this advice to our more modest goals, or perhaps, find the capital to do it in a big way. Especially important, check out her sample marketing plan!

Plan Your Marketing Strategy

By Kerry LePage

One of the elements most critical to any organization's long-term success is a strong marketing plan. It is also one of the most frequently neglected of all business-planning functions. The only way to assure your place in today's competitive marketplace is to know your product and your customers better than anyone else. Armed with this knowledge, you can develop a strong marketing plan for your organization.

If time is your enemy, consider hiring an outside consultant or agency to write your plan. In addition to giving your plan high priority, they have access to research and industry standards that will result in a stronger plan.

We all know that the marketplace is not getting any easier on us. A strong marketing plan is your road map to the 21st century.

Let's Look at a Marketing Plan

Each organization is unique, but following is a basic outline of a solid marketing plan:

I. **Introduction**
   A. Situation Analysis (detailed sales reports, current market share, etc.)
   B. Short-Term Business Goals (be specific, e.g. "increase sales for Product X by ten percent" this year)
   C. Long-Term Business Goals (e.g., "become the market leader in the Product X category by the year 2001")

II. **Marketing Analysis** (by product line and/or service line)
   A. Target Market(s)
      1. Who is our customer? (describe overall market and demographics of current/potential customers)
   B. Four Ps Analysis
      1. Product (what are we selling? describe each product/service in detail)
      2. Price (what price—might not be monetary—do we charge?)
      3. Place (where is our product distributed?)
      4. Promotion (how do we promote our product?)
   C. Competitive Analysis (other organizations and/or behaviors)
   D. S.W.O.T. Analysis (strengths/weaknesses/opportunities/threats—this should be a team effort of employees, customers, vendors and other key audiences)

III. **Organizational Identity/Position Statement**
   A. Develop or refine position statement to accurately reflect your organization's products/services as they relate to marketing analysis
      1. Should have an underlying emotional pull
      2. Should be short and memorable (e.g., McDonald's "you deserve a break today")

IV. Marketing Program Elements (how we are going to achieve our goals)

  A. Objectives (e.g., awareness, increase market share, increase sales of a specific product, etc.)

  B. Advertising/Promotion

    1. Consumer and trade advertising/promotion

      a. Analysis of different media/recommendations

      b. Budget/timeline

    2. Collateral materials (brochures, newsletters, catalogs, etc.)

      a. Analysis/recommendations

      b. Budget/timeline

    3. Direct mail

      a. Analysis/recommendations

      b. Budget/timeline

  C. Public Relations

    1. Story ideas/other opportunities/recommendations

    2. Budget/timeline

  D. Customer Retention

    1. Review of current program/recommendations

    2. Budget/timeline

  E. Special Events/Trade Shows/Conferences, etc.

    1. Review of existing and potential special events/recommendations

    2. Budget/timeline

  F. Fundraising and/or Sponsorship

    1. Review of current program/recommendations

    2. Budget/timeline

  G. Other Promotional Opportunities

    1. Internet, specialty items, etc.

V. Evaluation

  A. Market Research

    1. Primary research/recommendations (e.g., you hire a market-research firm to conduct a customer survey)

    2. Secondary research/recommendations (e.g., you access market research produced by other organizations)

B. Measurement

    1. Develop goals and qualitative/quantitative evaluation mechanisms for each promotional activity (in other words, how are we going to track the results of our investment?)

Now that you understand the key elements of your marketing plan, let's look in-depth at the many ways you can market your product or service. This section will review each of the marketing-program elements outlined in the marketing plan. Follow these guidelines to make sure your marketing investment pays off.

Print Advertising Guidelines

Placing an ad in a publication one or two times is not going to increase sales significantly. There are several factors that go into effective print advertising.

Step 1: Decide what type of print media is best for your needs. With print, you have a variety of options: magazines, newspapers, Yellow Pages, newsletters, and circulars.

There are two categories of print media available: trade and consumer publications. Trade publications target corporate buyers of products and services. They typically offer lower rates due to their smaller circulation. If your organization's sales are strictly business-to-business, trade advertising may be all you need.

Consumer publications, with subscribers and newsstand sales, offer an extremely well-qualified audience. Because of this and their larger circulation, you will pay a higher price for ad space. Rates will vary drastically among publications, so be sure to get a media kit and study the demographics, circulation, and rates of each one.

Step 2: Develop a budget and a media plan. Print is usually the least-expensive medium. Collect media kits and back issues from the various publications you are considering. Call advertisers in the publication and ask them how well it has worked for them.

Next, find out what the average for advertising spending is in your industry and start developing a budget. Don't forget to include production costs for your ads in your budget. Each publication you advertise in will probably require ad film or camera-ready art for your ad.

Step 3: Decide where and when you want to advertise. Follow these rules when making your decisions:

- Remember, frequency is the key to success with all types of advertising. Think of advertising as an investment. Commit to at least a six-month trial, and don't cancel your advertising when your phone doesn't ring right away. A study by the Advertising Research Foundation and the American Business Press shows that one product advertised at medium levels over twelve months experienced a sales increase of eighty percent. Experience is the only way to find out what kind of sales increase you can expect.

- Choose size over color. Although color attracts attention, it isn't cost effective. Tests show that color is unnecessary in four out of five ads. Run a larger ad instead.

- Depending on your budget, it pays to hire an expert media buyer. This is especially important when buying radio and television ads. Media buyers have greater leverage due to their high volume of ads. They will recommend the best publications, write your media plan, negotiate the best rates, and ensure good placement of your ad. Media buyers normally work on a commission basis.

- The commission amount depends on several factors, but fifteen percent is a safe estimate.

- Be aware of media commissions. A fifteen percent commission for advertising agencies/media-buying services is usually built into advertising rates. Publications may let you take the fifteen percent commission if you place the advertising yourself. It won't hurt to ask!

- Don't work from the rate card. Depending on the available ad space a publication has, it may give you a lower rate than published if you commit to an advertising schedule. Additionally, ask the publication about any "remnant" ads—in spaces that become available at press time; prices are usually well below the rate card.

Step 4: Create your ad(s).

If you are visually oriented and don't have the budget to hire someone, you can create your own ad. Look for ideas in ads that you like, then create an ad on page-layout software. If possible, have a marketing or graphics professional critique the ad for you.

Check the publication's specifications to find out what kind of finished artwork you must provide. Sometimes, all they need is a high-resolution laser print. If they need ad film, go to a service bureau for help.

Remember these rules as you create your ad(s):

- Don't clutter your ad with too much information. An ad is not a brochure. Keep this in mind as you or anyone else writes copy. Stick to one clear, memorable message that emphasizes your unique selling points.

- Include a high-quality photo or illustration to draw attention to your ad. The visual element should tie in with your message.

- Increase your ad's effectiveness by including an offer that requires the reader to act now. For instance, "Place an order by August 31 and receive 15% off!" Ask callers how they heard about you when they call, and track the responses by publication name and date. Try varying the offers among different publications to test their effectiveness.

- "Free" is still one of the most powerful words in the English language.

- Keep your copy crisp and clean. Eliminate extra words wherever possible.

- Remember, your ad is the first impression of you that customers get. If your budget allows, hire a copywriter and graphic designer to create your ad. The investment will pay off in increased sales.

How Much Money Should You Spend On Advertising?

As a general rule, you should allocate a specific percentage of your sales to advertising. Here are some industry averages.

Business Type	Advertising (as a percentage of sales)
Auto Dealers	1.6
Auto Service/Repair	3.4
Department Stores	3.5
Finance Services	2.5
Gas Stations	1.6
Hospitals	3.2
Hotels/Motels	3.5
Movie Theaters	4.1
Personal Services	7.5
Photo Labs	4.7
Renting & Leasing	2.5
Real Estate Agents	1.7
Restaurants	3.7
Retail Stores (general)	4.2
Specialty Contractors	1.9

Radio & TV Advertising

Most small- to medium-sized businesses believe that radio and television advertising is not for them. It's too expensive. The audience reach is too broad. Other advertising options are a better fit, they think.

Although this view used to be true, "the times, they are a-changin'." With the advent of cable television, along with radio's very targeted program formats, you can reach an extremely targeted audience through broadcast advertising.

Target Audience   Know whom you want to reach. Who buys your product or service? The better you know your consumer, the better job your media buyer can do.

Radio and cable television offer a very targeted audience. For example, programs such as "The X Games" deliver a young audience of nine- to 25-year-olds who are looking for extreme forms of entertainment. Unlike network TV, cable TV can be tailored to specific geographic areas. You can advertise in specific metropolitan areas, such as Tempe, Arizona, or reach a particular region of the country, through a series of interconnects linking cable systems nationwide.

Price   Even though cable TV has made television more affordable than ever before, you still need to invest enough money to generate response to your ad. You should have $50,000+ to spend if you want to consider a television campaign. Plan to invest at least $10,000 in radio time if you are advertising in a major market.

Use a professional media buyer to place any broadcast advertising. Their expertise and knowledge of rates, reach, and media options will more than pay for their modest fee. And because media buyers work for a variety of clients, they have buying power that your business can never achieve. The bottom line is that they can negotiate a better deal for you.

Creative End   Because they generate higher responses than other forms of advertising, radio and television are very cluttered advertising media. Cutting corners on the creative end will do more harm than good, especially in the "high touch" medium of TV. Statistics show that people do not register 85 percent of the commercial messages they see every day. Of the remaining 15 percent, five percent are "so irritating that they are counterproductive." That means you have a one in ten chance of actually influencing your target audience to act. No other medium does that as well as television.

You should work with an advertising agency or a professional producer to develop your radio and TV ads. Production costs for professionally produced sixty-second radio spots range from $1500 to $3500. Television-production costs vary wildly, depending on such factors as the concept of your spot, who produces it, and how many paid actors are involved. You can spend anywhere from $10,000 to $100,000 for a thirty-second spot.

The production process for a TV commercial goes like this. Once you have approved the initial concept(s) from your advertising team, they will create a storyboard, which looks like a cartoon drawing of your commercial. They will use that storyboard to get bids from production companies and directors who will actually shoot your spot(s). It usually takes two to five days to shoot a commercial, depending on such details as the number of locations and casting needs.

Produce at least two different spots within your campaign so you can test different messages. This will also keep your audience from getting bored. The production costs of your second spot will be significantly lower, since you can combine both spots into the same shoot.

Some advertisers have had success purchasing "canned" spots and customizing them for their local market. Many manufacturers offer these spots at no charge to their retailers, for instance. These canned spots can save significantly on your production costs.

Collateral Materials (brochures, newsletters, catalogs, etc.)
Many businesses find that printed materials are all they need to promote their products. A strong catalog, newsletter, or brochure, combined with trade shows, publicity campaigns, and word-of-mouth advertising, can make all the difference in your sales.

Here are some guidelines for producing a successful newsletter (most of this advice is relevant to *all* printed materials).

Newsletters are one of the most cost-effective and entertaining ways to inform your target audience about your company or organization. Their news format lends interest and credibility to your message. Combined with photos, illustrations, and an attractive layout, they can be an excellent way to present and reinforce your message.

Thanks to today's sophisticated desktop-publishing software, most organizations produce at least one newsletter. It's great to have Sally in public relations whip out this month's edition. Or is it?

Producing a high-quality newsletter requires many skills. You must be a strong journalistic writer, decent photographer, graphic designer, editor, and print-production expert all rolled into one. On top of that, you need to search for story ideas and plan for future issues.

An effective newsletter—one that will be read, remembered, and appreciated—takes more than one person. It also takes planning. If you want your newsletter to produce significant results, take the time to accomplish the following:

1. **Establish your objective.**

   What is the goal of your newsletter? Do you want to inform current and potential customers about your business? Or is it an internal publication for your employees? Know what you want your newsletter to achieve and keep it in mind as you develop articles.

2. **Identify your audience.**

   Who are your readers? What is their average age/education level/ethnic background, etc.? Should you produce a multilingual newsletter? Knowing your audience is critical.

3. **Determine publication size/frequency.**

   Determine how long the newsletter needs to be and how often you should publish it. Don't be too ambitious. After the novelty wears off, it gets more burdensome to produce a weekly, monthly, or even bimonthly publication—and it may be unnecessary. Ask your audience how often they'd like to hear from you.

4. **Provide useful information.**

We are all bombarded with information these days. So don't fill the pages of your newsletter with meaningless fluff or blatant self-promotion. If you want your readers to value your newsletter, pack it with information they can't get elsewhere. Take the time to research articles, interview key personnel, and provide facts, figures, and examples. Develop regular columns as appropriate. Ask your readers for contributions. Enhance your stories with sidebars, crisp photos, clip art, and illustrations.

5. **Research other publications.**

Start collecting samples of newsletters—good and bad—and notice what works well and what doesn't. Here are some examples of excellent newsletters:

- *Communication Briefings*—Phone (703) 548-3800; 1101 King St., Suite 110, Alexandria, VA 22314
- *The Ragan Report*—Phone (312) 922-8245; 407 S. Dearborn, Chicago, IL 60605
- *Bottom Line Personal*—Phone (800) 274-5611; P.O. Box 58446, Boulder, CO 80322
- *John Naisbitt's Trend Letter*—Phone (800) 368-0115; c/o Global Network, Dept. NEC102, 1101 30th St. NW, Washington, DC 20007

6. **Calculate production costs.**

Does your newsletter really need to be full-color? Many excellent newsletters are printed with just two ink colors. However, if you must have several ink colors, you can save significantly by printing "shells" of your newsletter in color. These shells contain your basic design that remains unchanged with each issue, such as the masthead, epitaph, and borders. You then imprint each issue with your stories and photos in just one or two ink colors. If your quantities are small, you can print out the issues on a high-resolution Postscript laser printer or even make photocopies onto your shells.

Choose your paper stock carefully—and don't change it unless you have to. Paper is a subtle, but important, part of your overall design. Print on recycled paper stock if possible.

Another important production cost is postage. Make sure your mailing list is carefully targeted and up-to-date. If your budget allows, print "address correction requested" on your newsletter to make sure you get all address changes that are registered with the post office.

7. **Invest in good writing and design.**

   Newsletter writing has a style all its own. Hire someone who has experience writing in this medium. Invest in good design, as well. Your newsletter should reflect your organization's identity and mission. Keep the design simple and allow for white space—you don't want your newsletter to look like it was laid out with a crowbar.

   A cost-saving technique is to have a graphic designer develop a basic design template in a desktop-publishing program such as PageMaker, QuarkXPress, or Ventura Publisher. Then you or your staff can lay out the newsletter in the future. You should have the graphic designer review the final layout for each issue, just to make sure you haven't made any design mistakes.

8. **Consider electronic publishing.**

   With the cost of paper and postage skyrocketing, now is the time to consider publishing your newsletter electronically. If your audience is networked and/or linked to the Internet, this can be an extremely cost-effective option. You can publish your newsletter as straight text and send it out as e-mail, or use the more sophisticated software now available to produce publications on the World Wide Web. Check the latest computer magazines to find out more about electronic publishing, or ask your favorite computer guru.

9. **Get feedback.**

   Don't produce your newsletter in a vacuum. One good reality check is to ask yourself and your readers whether they'd subscribe to your newsletter. Also, conduct annual readership surveys to make sure you're still meeting readers' needs. Let readers know the changes you're making as a result of their suggestions.

10. **Reap the rewards.**

    Newsletters are an important marketing tool. Invest the time and money it takes so that your newsletter produces bottom-line results for your organization.

Direct Mail

A direct mail program requires a long-term commitment.
If your phone doesn't ring off the hook when you send out 1,000 postcards to new prospects, don't throw in the towel. It takes a minimum of three exposures to your message to generate a response. And even then, a one- to five-percent response rate is considered an average return rate for direct mail.

Tailor your communication to each customer or prospect.
Don't offer them products or services you know they don't need. Make your offer relevant to them. Personalize letters and mailing labels whenever possible.

Develop and maintain a customer database.
If you don't have a database of customers and prospects, hire a marketing database expert immediately. You can also build your

own—invest in a good database book and software that will grow with your company. Some good resources:

- Harvey Mackay's "Mackay 66" list of customer information—see *Swim with the Sharks Without Getting Eaten Alive*, p. 45–53
- *eMarketing* by Seth Rodin
- *Direct Magazine*, phone (203) 358-9900
- The Cowles Report on Database Marketing (800) 775-3777
- *Database Marketing* by Edward Nash
- The Direct Marketing Association, based in New York, with chapters nationwide.

Know your customer(s).
Analyze your sales records and segment your customers by lifetime sales value if at all possible. At a minimum, know your different customers' demographics and buying habits so that you can customize promotions to meet their needs.

Integrate direct mail with other marketing methods.
Be there for your customers with information and service through as many channels of communication as possible. Don't rely on direct mail alone to carry your messages; supplement it with paid advertising, public relations, newsletters, and other efforts.

Ask the right questions.
As you collect information for your customer database, be sure you are asking the right questions to gather information you can act on. Nobody likes to waste time in today's hurry-up world.

Don't cut corners on any component of your direct mailing.
Invest in a good mailing list if you don't already have one. There are a variety of sources for mailing lists—check your Yellow Pages or call the local chapter of the American Marketing Association. Develop several strong incentives for each type of customer. Finish the sale with strong copy, headlines, and graphics.

Take the time to test your offer.
Before you send out 10,000 pieces, send a test group of 1,000. If you don't get a one- to five-percent response, pull the offer and try another one. You should also consider testing a variety of offers to each audience segment.

Track your responses and keep a regular mailing schedule.
This is easy to put off—but don't! Hire someone to manage your customer database if necessary. You can hire a freelancer for a lot less than the cost of missed opportunities.

Direct Mail "Trade Secrets"

- Merge/purge names. Names that appear on two or more lists can be made into a list that almost always outperforms any single list from which these names were drawn. (In other words, people who appear on multiple mailing lists are excellent targets.)

- Overlays (also called "enhancements") on purchased lists, such as lifestyle characteristics, income, education, propensity to respond to direct mail offers, will greatly improve response.

- Offers that ask for a "Yes or No" response get more orders than those that don't.

- A time limit on your offer will improve response.

- Free gifts outperform discount offers.

- Self-mailers are less expensive to produce, but envelope mailings draw more response.

- The longer you can keep prospects reading your letter, the more likely it is that they will respond. (So that's why direct mailings have so many pieces inside!)

- Credit-card acceptance and a toll-free number are a must for consumer orders.

Public Relations

Other sections of this book are dedicated to this subject. A solid public-relations plan, when integrated with a paid promotional campaign, are the mainstays of any successful marketing effort.

Customer Retention— or "Relationship Marketing"

By now, you've probably read the statistics. Attracting new customers is incredibly expensive as advertising costs skyrocket. In 1965, the cost of a thirty-second national TV spot was $19,700; today, it runs upward of $100,000.

As media outlets become more and more fragmented, advertisers are forced to spread their dollars out to get the numbers they need to reach new customers. Faced with a dizzying array of options, customers are beginning to realize that Brand X isn't the only one for them. "Marketers are facing a new skepticism. Years of scams, lousy products, inferior service, and advertising overkill have led many consumers to be leery of almost any new product. More and more, we're relying on the people and the businesses we trust to deliver the product," notes Seth Rodin, author of the book *eMarketing*.

Meanwhile, consider these numbers (taken from After-Marketing—How to Keep Customers for Life Through Relationship Marketing by Terry G. Vavra):

- Sixty-five percent of the average company's business comes from its current, satisfied customers.

- It costs five times as much to acquire a new customer as it costs to service an existing customer.

- Ninety-one percent of unhappy customers will never again buy from that company, and they will tell at least nine other people about their experience.

We have reached the age of "relationship marketing." The traditional marketing model (define your target market and promote an existing or new product to it), also called "conquest marketing," has been superseded by such terms as "micromarketing," "database marketing," "customer intimacy," and more. Today, the focus is on gaining customer share rather than market share.

So how do you do this? A customer database is the first step. Amazingly enough, many companies still lack any significant information on their customers. The power of a strong customer database is certainly impressive.

Here are a few examples, taken from *eMarketing*:

- Long-distance heavyweight MCI started its Friends & Family program for existing customers. By encouraging them to start their own calling circle and save on long-distance costs, they solidified relationships with existing customers and attracted new customers at the same time.

- The Ritz-Carlton hotel chain quietly maintains a customer database that keeps track of every habit or preference a guest displays. Which hotel services did they use? What food or beverages did they order through room service? Guests who stayed in Phoenix a few months ago will find that wine delivered to their room in New York comes with a glass of ice on the side, because the Ritz knows that's they way they like it. Talk about making a customer feel special. American Airlines has a similar database approach—passengers who log a lot of miles with them get a special flag when their record shows up on the computer, no matter where they are in the world—"treat this customer with extra care."

- Coca-Cola has built a database on its 300,000 fountain customers, identifying the attitudes and needs of each, from fast-food restaurants to convenience stores. The database constantly measures the customer's satisfaction level, so that every marketing effort and sales call addresses that customer's needs and interests. Because Coca-Cola has the customer's merchandising history, Coke can help that customer anticipate situations and increase sales at key buying times.

How can you translate this success to your organization? Following are some basic how-tos. Once you commit to a program, bring in database and marketing experts to help you implement it.

Step 1: Commit to developing a strong company culture for your customer-loyalty program. You must love your products less and your customers more. Realize that if your competitors have a customer database and you don't, they have a sustainable competitive advantage.

Step 2: Allocate a budget based on the impact of customer retention on profitability. Study your sales reports to determine who your most profitable customers are. Note that the key word is profitable—just because you have a big customer doesn't mean that customer is your most profitable account.

Step 3: Segment your customers into appropriate categories for your business. An example is: 1) User—has purchased your product at least once; 2) Customer—has purchased your product repeatedly; 3) Advocate—your very best, most-loyal customers. Note that these customers are an excellent resource for referral programs and other incentives targeted directly at them.

Step 4: Develop your database. There are a number of good off-the-shelf database programs out there—or you may need a custom database. Either way, take the time to build it right. There are dozens of books on how to develop a good customer database. For trade customers, refer to Harvey Mackay's book, *Swim with the Sharks Without Being Eaten Alive,* for his "Mackay's 66" list of information you should have on your customers. Consumer databases are inherently more limited, but be sure to gather as much demographic, geographic, and psychographic information as possible.

Step 5: Once you have a working database and a good idea of your different customer segments, start testing different promotions for each. For instance, a coupon promotion can turn "users" into "customers." A newsletter can be developed for "customers" and "advocates." Edward L. Nash notes, in his book *Database*

Marketing—The Ultimate Marketing Tool: "A good customer loyalty program is based around customer service, extended into tangible reminders of the expertise of the seller. By this I mean sending brochures, articles, bulletins, samples—information that offers news of products and applications, or references that will help the customer be more successful at his or her job. Certainly one of the best examples of this approach is the creation of newsletters and even magazines, provided they are perceived as helpful and of obvious value."

Step 6: Evaluate and retool your program as needed. Market research—formal or informal—is a critical part of your program. Plan to survey customers regularly to determine whether your products and programs are still what they need.

A good, consistent customer-loyalty program will pay off in increased sales and profitability. Your advertising will be more targeted and your sales promotions and public-relations efforts will be more successful.

Examples of Relationship Marketing Programs

Program Type	Example
Frequent purchaser prizes/rewards	Airline mileage programs
Discounts	Coupons/Rebates
Reminders	Time to clean your carpet/clean your teeth...
New products	What new products do you need from us?
Predict future habits/co-market	You just bought a house from us. Here's a discount on furniture at a store near you.
Offer resources	Provide useful information to your customers that will help them live better/do their job better, etc.

Special Events/Trade Shows/Conferences

Develop a list of consumer and trade special events that you or your company will attend this year. Develop a specific goal for each event and track your success at meeting your goal. Goals are not always simply "collect 100 new business leads;" they are also, "meet with 50 percent of our current customers to show them our new products;" "practice new sales technique with all customers who visit our booth," etc. At regular intervals, evaluate the results of each event. Many will fail to measure up from a "new business cards" perspective alone; be sure to consider other criteria before eliminating it from your lineup.

Other Promotional Opportunities

The explosive growth of the Internet is an opportunity no one can ignore. Invest in a home page, keep it updated, and make sure you're listed on the major search engines. Check out the many articles (including those in this book) and books on the topic for more details.

Don't forget specialty items as a way to build goodwill and recognition for your product. Pens, magnets, Post-it notes, and more can really go a long way to keep you in a customer's mind. Be sure to invest in good-quality items that are useful and/or tie in with your message and your product somehow. For instance, a book promoter could give away bookmarks, page magnifiers, Post-it notes, etc. as tie-ins.

If you have to pay for it, it's not publicity, it's advertising. Publicity is THE economical way to get the word out about your book. Joan Stewart gives another perspective on how to get more of it.

The Top Three Ways to Snag Valuable Free Publicity: Write, Speak, and Schmooze with the Media

By Joan Stewart

Of the hundreds of ways you can self-promote your product, service, cause, or issue, these are my three favorites:

- **Writing** how-to or advice articles for newsletters, newspapers, magazines, and trade publications gives you instant credibility. Often, the articles attract the attention of reporters, who may then ask to interview you for a feature story.

- **Public speaking** also offers a gold mine of promotional opportunities and helps establish you as an expert in your field. Scared of public speaking? So are most other people. But professional speakers will tell you that the more you speak, the more you can teach the butterflies in your stomach to fly in formation. Once you get the hang of it, speaking is fun. So is the resulting publicity.

- **Schmoozing** with the media also pays huge dividends. The secret is for you to establish yourself as a golden news source and make yourself invaluable to busy reporters, editors, and radio talk-show hosts.

Here's how to do it.

Write, Write, Write

Editors want articles that will inspire, educate, calm, enlighten, humor, and entertain their readers. They want advice from you that will help readers find more time, save money, feel healthier, look thinner, be safer, and have better sex lives. And they rely on people like you to provide them.

1. Call the advertising department of every newspaper and magazine you want to get into and ask for a copy of their editorial calendar. It's a free listing of all the special topics and special sections coming up during the calendar year. It will tip you off to sections where your article would be a good fit, so you can query the editor weeks and even months ahead.

2. Call, write or e-mail the editor with a suggested topic you want to write about. The best topics are those that discuss a problem the audience is having, and ways to solve it.

3. National magazines often have writer's guidelines at their website.

4. Don't balk at giving away free information. Editors won't be interested in your article unless it's helpful. Besides, just think about how much money you would have to pay if you bought the same amount of newspaper space where your article is going to be printed for free. However, offer your article free to an editor only on the condition you can include an identifier paragraph at the end telling readers how to get in touch with you. If editors won't agree to include this paragraph, don't give them the article unless they are paying you their standard freelance fee.

5. The identifier paragraph should explain who you are, what you do, and how people can get in touch with you. Always include your website address. If you sell related resource materials such as books, tapes, or special reports, include that information, too.

6. In the identifier paragraph, consider a special offer. For example, "For a list of 20 tips on how to save money on taxes, fax your letterhead with the words 'Tax Tips' to me at (fax number)." Collect the information on those who respond and add it to your database.

7. Choose a catchy headline that lets the readers know you understand their pain and will make their lives easier. Example: "8 Mistakes You Don't Want to Make When Hiring an Attorney," "The Top 10 _____ Do's and Don'ts," "Quick _____ Tips to Use Now."

8. Offer a list of bulleted tips.

9. Write articles for industry newsletters. My favorite resource is the *Oxbridge Directory of Newsletters*, which lists more than 18,000 newsletters by topic and includes detailed information on the type of audience and subjects covered. Most larger libraries have this resource directory. The online version at **www.mediafinder.com/nlr_home.cfm** includes only basic information, as well as contact names and phone numbers. It's enough to get you started.

10. Write articles for electronic magazines and include a paragraph of information at the end that leads readers to your website. My favorite resource is John Labovitz's well-organized e-zine site at **www.meer.net/~johnl/e-zine-list**. You'll find more than 4,000 e-zines on more than 100 topics.

11. Whenever someone asks you to write for their electronic magazine or newsletter, visit their website first to see whether they have a resource section where you would be a good fit. Ask for a free link, in exchange for providing a free article.

12. When submitting articles, always include your professional business photo. If you don't have one, get one. You can have a business photo taken and about a dozen prints made for less than $75.

13. Recycle your articles. With a little editing, most articles can be recycled and customized to fit the needs of other publications. When you offer an article to an editor, be certain that you maintain all reprint rights. This lets you offer the piece to someone else. Editors who insist on maintaining all rights to the article should be willing to pay you at least several hundred dollars for it. If that's the case, get a written contract.

14. Make reprints. After your article is published, call the editor and, as a courtesy, ask permission to reprint it. Editors will almost always agree. Use the reprints at trade shows, as giveaways at your speaking engagements, tuck them into your media kit, send them along with query letters to reporters, and include them along with proposals you are submitting to clients.

15. Be fanatical about meeting deadlines. Miss one, and some editors won't have anything to do with you again.

16. Check all your facts. If an editor is forced to run a correction as a result of inaccurate information in your article, it may be the last time your name ever appears in that editor's publication.

17. Several months after an article appears, follow up with the editor and offer a piece on another topic.

Speak, Speak Speak

Public speaking is a superb way to get lots of free publicity and build instant credibility. Here are publicity tips for anyone who wants to get onto the speaking circuit—or is already there.

1. Scan your local newspapers, magazines, and trade publications for the names of groups you want to speak to. Call the

program directors, tell them what you speak about, and ask them to keep you in mind if they need a speaker or if someone who they already booked cancels.

2. Do not expect to receive a fee for your speaking if you haven't spoken before. Only after you learn platform skills and have been on the speaking circuit for several months should you consider asking for a fee. Besides, free speaking gives you valuable exposure.

3. Learn platform skills by joining your local Toastmasters.

4. Do not, under any circumstances, write a speech and read it word for word from the lectern. Rehearse your presentation so you can speak naturally and work only with notes. For a great resource on how to learn your material, check out the book *Wake 'Em Up* by Tom Antion at **www.Antion.com**. Also sign up for his free, biweekly newsletter *Great Speaking*.

5. Ask your host organization for permission to sell your book or other products from the back of the room. If they balk, tell them you will donate 20 percent of all sales to their group or their favorite charity. Then, be sure someone from the group announces that to the audience.

6. Once you are booked for a speaking engagement, ask the host organization if they are publicizing your presentation. If not, send out news releases yourself with their permission, particularly if the meeting is open to the public. Your professional business photo should accompany every news release.

7. Build your celebrity image by asking the host organization to display posters (which you will provide) in their meeting room several months before you speak. This builds anticipation.

8. Take a short, written introduction to the meeting with you and ask the person who introduces you to read it word for word. Be sure the introduction refers to you as an "expert" in your field.

9. Take something free to hand out to audience members. It should include your name and contact information. It can be a brochure, a bookmark, or a list of tips you're going to discuss in your presentation.

10. Take something to give away as a door prize after your speech. This gives you a good excuse to collect audience members' business cards, then add them to your database later.

11. Every time you speak before a group, offer to submit a short summary of your presentation for the group's newsletter. Don't forget to send your photo. It gets you in front of those you just spoke to as well as those who missed you the first time around. Many groups also send their newsletters to the media, so this is a great way to build credibility. Be sure the last paragraph in your article tells people what you do and how to get in touch with you. Include your website address.

12. Post your speaking engagements at your website, and mention topics you speak about.

13. Build a network of other speakers who concentrate on your topic or area of expertise. Agree informally that you will refer reporters to each other whenever the media calls. Often, reporters want more than one source for a story. It's a chance for all of you to get additional publicity. This is also a great way to keep program planners happy because you'll be able to refer them to a good substitute speaker if you have another commitment on the day they want you.

14. If you are doing an out-of-town speaking engagement, call the local newspaper where you will be speaking, tell them to whom you will be speaking, and ask if they would be interested in interviewing you. Do the same with local radio stations.

Schmooze, Schmooze, Schmooze with the Media

Dying to get to know the local columnist who writes for your favorite newspaper, or the reporter who covers your industry? Many people are intimidated by reporters and wouldn't think of approaching them. But smart publicity hounds always make the first move. Once reporters know you care, they will care about what you know—and maybe write about you. Here's a handy guide to schmoozing.

1. Invite the reporter for lunch or coffee. The restaurant needn't be fancy.

2. Become familiar with the reporter's stories, so you can discuss them and really make a good first impression. Most people don't do this and end up asking the reporter dumb questions like, "So what do you cover anyway?"

3. Bring a media kit or background information and offer it at the beginning of the lunch without a lot of explanation.

4. "Make nice" by first making small talk. Ask the reporter about his job, his family, and what he thinks about the top national story of the day.

5. Explain new trends you are seeing in your industry. The labor shortage, technology, and problems running a small business are hot topics. How are you dealing with them?

6. Let the reporter know all the areas in which you are an expert as well as areas in which you are not prepared to comment.

7. Ask about other subjects they cover or stories they are working on. You might know someone who can be a helpful source.

8. Never talk off the record to a reporter whom you have just met.

9. Ask about the reporter's personal interests, family, and hobbies. This is important information that you might use later when it's time to make another contact with the reporter.

10. You aren't expected to suggest story ideas, but if you can think of any, mention them. Never directly ask a reporter to write about you.

11. If a reporter writes about you and the story is fair and accurate, consider sending a hand-written thank-you note.

12. Never send a gift afterward. Most newspapers have ethics policies prohibiting reporters from accepting anything of value.

13. Offer your home telephone number, cell phone number, and beeper number. Invite the reporter to call you day or night. Promise to do your best to return phone calls quickly—then do it.

14. Pass along names of two or three other people you know who would make good contacts for the reporter, even if they are your competitors. (Bad-mouthing competitors, by the way, is tacky.)

15. Ask, "How else can I help you?"

16. Exchange business cards.

17. Don't grab the check. Either split it, or let the reporter pay for your meal. (Ethics policies again!)

18. Mail the thank-you note and any other information you promised within 24 hours.

19. Keep in touch regularly. Offer constructive feedback on their stories. Fax helpful articles about their areas of expertise or their hobbies. Share news tips and story ideas. Show them that you care, and they will continue to care about what you know.

20. Have lunch again in four to six months.

I recently read a newspaper feature story about Charlene Costanzo that mentioned that she was the author of a self-published book that had already sold more than 250,000 copies. I called her and asked her to consider writing a chapter for this book. She mentioned that she was starting her national book tour and probably wouldn't have the time to write in between the travel to various cities and the many signings and interviews. Since persistence is my middle name, we found a way to work together. I knew that I wanted to know more about the secrets that led to her success and I assumed you would, too.

On Raising Awareness and Building Good Will

By Charlene Costanzo

When it comes to promotion, I like to think in terms of "raising awareness and building goodwill" rather than "selling." Many people who are uncomfortable with the notion of selling can feel very reassured by the idea of building goodwill. Who doesn't want to build goodwill?

I first came to appreciate this approach during the years my sister-in-law and I co-owned and operated Tisket a Tasket, a gift-basket store in Jamestown, New York. We provided an alternative to sending flowers when people wanted to say "Congratulations," "Thank You," or "I Care" to their friends and families. Along with appropriate food, toiletries, and other contents, each basket contained a quote from literature or sacred writings that expressed meaningful emotion for the occasion. Because I believed so deeply in the quality of our products and the value of our service, it was easy for me to be enthusiastic about promoting it. It became natural for me to think, "How can I let people know, or remind them, about this wonderful service?" We used several methods to introduce the business and to continually build awareness afterward.

We began with a simple direct-mail letter that was sent to all our friends, family, and acquaintances. A news release and several follow-up calls to the local newspaper resulted in a feature article and photo on the front page of the lifestyle section. With that, we were off to a great start. Like most small businesses, we had a limited budget for advertising and did very little of it. We relied heavily on regular mailings to customers. Fortunately, word-of-mouth publicity helped our customer base grow. Soon, because of customer demand, we offered nationwide shipping, not just local delivery.

Gift recipients throughout the country then became customers themselves. Our gift fliers evolved into holiday catalogs.

Naturally, every time we introduced a new product or service, we notified the media with news releases. Sometimes our information got picked up, sometimes it didn't. Let's face it, sometimes our business news is just not newsworthy. Sometimes, however, the media find it of value because it is inspirational or entertaining. For example, when we designed our "Long Stemmed Chocolate Chip Cookies" as a gift for Valentine's Day, we sent our surprise rose boxes in advance of the holiday to each of the affiliate stations in our news area and ended up being a feature story throughout the day on February 14. However, I think it is important to recognize that it is not the media's job to help us promote our business and remember always to approach them with consideration of their time and respect for their perspective.

When vendors called Tisket a Tasket with products for us to consider, I appreciated those who did it with courtesy and enthusiasm and took the attitude that they were bringing helpful news to our attention rather than just "selling" us, as some vendors did. That experience reinforced my intention to promote my business in that spirit.

Making Contact

At the time of this writing, I am promoting my first book, *The Twelve Gifts of Birth*. On July 29, 1999, my husband, Frank, and I began a one-year tour throughout the country. As we shake, rattle, and roll down the highways and byways, signage on our motor home is raising awareness about *The Twelve Gifts of Birth* and our Polished Stone Tour. We will be visiting more than one hundred cities in which I have scheduled book signings and presentations in schools.

Living in a motor home and traveling throughout the country has been a dream of ours since we were married thirty years ago. There are many methods and approaches to promoting one's business, and I believe in choosing the style that reflects your values and the methods that you most enjoy. Try to find ways to incorporate your special interests and dreams into all aspects of your work.

For instance, one aspect of "raising awareness and creating good will" that I particularly enjoy is making courtesy calls, so I am always looking for reasons to make them. (And our trip will give me plenty of reason to make them.) When I have even a tentative radio interview scheduled, I contact several bookstores in the station's community. I introduce myself, determine whether I am calling at a convenient time, explain that I'm making a courtesy call simply to advise their store that there may be requests for my book and ask if they would like to hear about it. Approaching bookstores, especially the independents, with this spirit of helpfulness can be a very pleasant and effective experience. I know I appreciated this approach from vendors when I was a retailer years ago. If you have never used this approach, I encourage you to try it!

We were able to plan and execute our great adventure, in large part, because the book was already performing well, having sold 250,000 copies in less than a year after it was introduced on National Kids Day, September 19, 1998.

Word-of-mouth publicity has helped tremendously, as it did with Tisket a Tasket. We can't plan or control word-of-mouth publicity because it happens when people genuinely respond to a product or service and want to tell others. What we can control is the quality and care we put into our product or service. For me, publishing *The Twelve Gifts of Birth* was an act of love. In every aspect of its design and production, I sought beauty. Aim for the highest standards in your endeavor. Your customers will notice and appreciate it and help publicize it.

Research Your Market

Another critical step is one that should be taken even before you begin: market research. Go beyond your family and friends when you're trying to determine whether there's a market for your product. After all, their view is not objective. You need to know whether your book idea is really different. Does your neighborhood really need another frame shop? Is it likely your city will support the homemade dinner delivery service you are considering? Whatever product or service you dream of, follow your head as well as your heart. Do something you're enthusiastic about, but listen to the market. Make sure there's a need for what you have to offer.

Before I did my market research, I felt that expectant parents would be my top audience, and I was quite sure there was nothing else like *The Twelve Gifts of Birth* on the market. Was it true? I went to trade shows and called gift shops and bookstores. I asked them what the top-selling books aimed at expectant parents were, and found out that there really wasn't anything like my book out there. I made a dummy copy of the book and took it to gift shops and bookstores. Then, I asked the manager or owner if they would mind taking a look at it. When they obliged, I asked, "What do you think customer response will be?" The reactions were emotional and positive, so I knew I had a winner. I also sought their advice on pricing and any other features they thought might be important.

I also became a student of the publishing industry. Every step of the way, I was always asking questions of people who knew a little more than I did, so I could learn. I joined several small-press publishing associations, and read many how-to books, including the *Self-Publishing Manual* by Dan Poynter. I sought the best talent I could afford to help me design and illustrate the book. I wrote a marketing plan, and followed it. In the plan, I defined my mission, my market, how many books I would print, how I would handle publicity, and my sales objectives. Even before it was at the printers, I became as active as my energy would permit to raise awareness about the book and the story behind it.

Because I believed so strongly in the life-affirming message in my book, I began giving away gift cards that contained the text. I donated copies of the book to schools, shelters, libraries, and hospitals. I contacted organizations that promote the well-being of children and offered to be a resource. I sought and established distribution methods besides bookstores, such as catalogs and premium sales.

Be Open to New Ideas

Whatever your product or service, there are many ways to promote it. So become a student of your industry. Maintain an open attitude toward learning new things. I encourage you to develop a plan and stick with it, but be willing to try new things. One book I often refer to for new ideas and inspiration is *1,001 Ways to Promote Your Book,* by John Kremer.

In all your efforts, maintain enthusiasm. If you want to be successful at promotion, set a minimum number of new contacts you want to make each day—whether they're major or minor contacts doesn't matter, just make contacts every day. Nurture a positive attitude even when the media is uninterested or an idea bombs.

I've heard many people say they are reluctant to promote themselves. Sometimes, as a result, they avoid promotional activities, and the endeavor suffers. If you catch yourself saying anything negative about your attitude or promotional abilities (like "I'm not very good at promotion"), I encourage you to add "until now" or "yet." It's helpful advice I picked up from *Building Your Field of Dreams* by Mary Mannin Morrissey, another book that helped me throughout the process of publishing and promoting my book.

Best wishes in building your dream!

How many of us dread getting on the phone to new people? Carol Starr makes "cold calls" (unsolicited promotional calls) to new people every day. Carol offers some user-friendly advice on how to take the chill out of cold calling. Cold calls and networking, she says, have made her business, Starr Gift Baskets, a success. She tells you how.

Ring Up Future Sales on the Phone

By Carol Starr

"Hi, I am Carol Starr with Starr Gift Baskets..."

This is my opening line for all sales and inquiry calls, the initial words to achieve my goal of a successful call. A successful call paves the road to a future sale and to developing a relationship with the person on the line.

I have been in the gift-basket business for ten years in Phoenix, Arizona; San Diego, California; and now in Houston, Texas. I guess I am an expert in starting new businesses.

I started my business in Houston eight years ago in my home, and I didn't know a single person here. Through networking, cold calling, and perseverance, we have developed a busy and profitable business.

I have written a book about gift baskets that has been out for eight years. Along with gift baskets, I also sell promotional products and am in the process of developing a new baby gift. I also have given many seminars at major gift shows throughout the United States.

I teach many gift-basket hopefuls who think creativity is where it's at. I change all their thinking with my nuts-and-bolts solutions to marketing. Sell first and then create!

I practice what I preach and make cold calls every day, and I try to get out for as many sales meetings as I am able. In my spare time, I ride a motorcycle, play racquetball, and am attempting to learn the piano.

But let's get back to the telephone and how to use it as a marketing tool.

Rules I Live By When Telephoning

I never, never, never sell on the phone: I open the door for future contacts.

Always introduce yourself first, especially when calling businesses. This saves the person who answers from having to ask who you're trying to reach and why you're calling.

The most important thing to do *when starting* a telephone-marketing campaign is to divert the attention of the person at the other end of the line from the reason for your call, regardless of his/her position with the company. Any time you can establish rapport with the person answering the phone, it will open the door for continued contact. That person will get to know you and your cheery personality and sense of humor—and look forward to your next call.

This does not mean engaging in long conversations. We all know the feeling of irritation from the many solicitation calls we get daily—so keep it short! Give the people on the other end of the line the right buzzwords to make them ask you questions. Thus, they won't see you as a pesky telemarketer. This is important because the person answering the phone could easily become a true benefactor for marketing your book or product and get you in contact with the right person at that company. Coming in cold, you never know just how much influence the person who answers the phone has.

The Proper Approach

What should we say or not say in order to be most effective and successful on the telephone?

Diversion is your biggest and best tool for overcoming those first five seconds of possible resistance on the other end of the telephone. You don't want the person answering the phone to know you're selling right away.

So here are three good things not to do:

1. Don't ask the person how he or she is. That'll immediately tell the person you are selling. Besides, you should always respect the fact that he or she may be busy or in a bad mood (and thus may not want to answer the question).

2. Never ask for the decision-maker, president, owner, or manager. This is another giveaway that you're selling something.

3. Don't allow any background noises to be heard. There is nothing more offensive than that "boiler room" atmosphere.

Your success rate can be pretty high as long as you are completely aware of the purpose of your call. Remember, you're not selling but opening the door to future contacts. So the purpose of the initial call may only be to find out to whom you can send your information, or the best time to call the key person, or maybe to find out the best way to present your material.

I always decide ahead of time what my purpose is. It could be to send out information or to drop off a gift and brochure, or just to find out if the company is looking to buy gifts for the next holiday.

Here are my two best openers:

"Hi, I am Carol Starr of Starr Gift Baskets, and I have a quick question for you, 'Do you people ever send gifts?'" I get many responses: "Yes," "A few," "Never," or "Let me put you in touch with the person who makes that decision." When I say "I have a quick question," it seems as though anyone who answers the phone is curious to know what the question is, and thus will stay on the phone to answer it.

Next scenario:

"Hi, I am Carol Starr with Starr Gift Baskets, and I would love to send you a brochure. Who is the best person to send it to?" I generally get a name, and then I add, "Do you give gifts to clients or those on your personal list very often?" I have said all I need to say in a matter of seconds. Again, no selling. No one is going to buy from a phone call, anyway. You are laying the groundwork for future business.

Professional telemarketers charge up to $35 an hour and will not have nearly the success that you will with this simple little method.

With calls like these, I'm developing my customer and hot potential business client list. I put the name on my customer-manager program (if you don't have one, you can make a simple list), and arrange for follow-up calls. This is simple and very painless, with very little rejection. I stay in charge and select the customers with the most potential this way. When I make my calls, I often feel like an actress on stage. It is really fun—honestly.

This is also a wonderful way to market your book or any product. Getting on the phone is great for seeking important information and potential business. It also sharpens your telephone persona. Besides that, this is also a very inexpensive marketing and sales plan.

Know Your Customers

Always keep in mind your desired end result, whether it be publicity, sales, or information dispersion, and be aware of who your best customer is.

For my gift-basket business, my best customers are companies such as property managers, car dealers, builders, and health-care facilities that have a regular use for gifts.

For my book and seminars, my best customers are people who want to go into the gift-basket business.

For my baby product, my best customers are individuals buying gifts for babies, or stores that want to carry my gift.

I have to tailor my approach to each of these markets. When it comes to my special products and book, I am a sort of mass marketer. However, with my gift-basket business, I market to one customer at a time. I cannot afford to send out gift-basket mailers by the thousands, so I make individual sales calls—lots of cold calls and follow-up calls. One customer in my gift-basket business can change the entire bottom line, so it's worth it to work this way. On the other hand, one new customer for my products or books just would not make a dent.

Give this issue of knowing your customer a lot of thought before planning your marketing strategy. Is your audience tightly targeted, semi-targeted, or the general public? This will help you decide what magazines, publications, and electronic media to pursue.

For instance, to market my new book and a new baby product I am just producing, I am attempting to think as globally as possible. I have begun to update all my reference books for TV and radio shows, magazines that are pertinent, and any other sources that I think would make or reach a good target audience. When selecting catalogs and magazines that might feature your book or product, check what price range and what products would interest them and what special audiences they reach.

When I began my marketing plan for my first book, *The How Tos of Gift Baskets*, I sent out a conservative one hundred information sheets. I sent them to business-opportunity magazines, directories, book reviewers, catalogs, business radio, and TV shows.

My results were varied. I got listed in several directories, and really lucked out with one particular magazine, *Small Business Opportunities*. I have been written up at least a dozen times over the past several years. This has helped to sell quite a few books. I also constantly explore the possibility of writing columns for several key publications, which also results in sales for my book. This type of writing establishes you as an authority on your topic.

I also wrote a letter to one of the major book chains and as a result, the chain made an initial purchase of several hundred copies. Since then, a number of new books on the gift-basket business have hit the market and have made it difficult to sell my second book to them. However, my first book is still the top-selling gift-basket book in their stores.

Use Time and Money Efficiently

Time and budget are the words of the day. You always want to use your time most effectively and efficiently. I do all of my marketing during business hours, and take care of my busy work before or after work hours.

I almost never set up an appointment because calling companies that have only an occasional use for gifts is not a wise use of my time. Besides, appointment times are difficult to set up, and when you do set one up, you always have too much or too little time before and after the appointment. I'm convinced that appointments are not the best use of your time, particularly if you are a one-person operation.

The exception to this rule is when *I am personally asked* to bring a potential customer some samples for a particular occasion or on-going use.

To save bucks and energy when seeking publicity or sources to sell your book, start out by sending an information sheet about your book or product. Make sure it contains a note that asks if they would be interested in a copy or sample. If the topic interests them, they will let you know and ask for a sample.

Take advantage of the Internet for information sources: catalogs, publishers, customers, and any other source you think might be useful. This will save you time and money as well.

Your Personality Counts

I think your marketing and sales effort has to go along with your basic personality. I like sending out lots of stuff and then waiting and hoping. Some people are very organized and oriented to seeing through one task at a time. Organization is definitely not my strong point.

Where Will You Sell?

I am currently working out all the possible places to sell my new baby item. I have divided my audience into groups. There are retail customers and wholesale customers, including other gift-basket companies.

I will reach my retail customers by:

1. Setting up a mall website (choice mail)
2. Sending information sheets to magazines and catalogs;
3. Displaying my product on shopping TV networks;
4. A postcard mailing, if I get a good enough response from a local trial mailing to friends and business associates.

I will reach the retail market through wholesale sources by:

1. Sending postcards to baby stores;
2. Displaying it in showrooms in city marketplaces and trade centers;
3. Taking the product around to local stores and hospital gift shops; and
4. Suggesting to hospitals that they give it as a gift for all new babies.

All I need to accomplish these goals is:

1. A prototype of the gift;
2. Picture postcards with the pertinent information for retail and wholesale customers;
3. An information sheet.

Be creative when you're looking for places to sell. If you're selling a book, maybe you could try a non-bookstore: grocery stores, gift shops, hardware stores. Whatever your subject, why not go after the source of products? Maybe you can work out a deal with a store to use your book as a premium.

Be Persistent

I do believe that sometimes we fail to succeed because we give up way too soon or too easily. Why not send a promotional letter to Oprah Winfrey? You never know when a topic is going to hit her as something she wants to explore. I gave up too soon with her and, sure enough, another gift-basket business got on her show. Can you imagine the thousands of books I would have sold if I hadn't given up?

You never know when or where your next break will come, so keep the lines of communication open. In business, I try to stay in touch with people three ways:

1. By telephone (three times a year);
2. By mail (send postcards with holiday information or just humor);
3. In person (always bring a gift when making a call, even if you are not in the gift business).

E-mail and faxes are also great for staying in touch.

Consistency and tenacity are my favorite words. I stress them regularly to attendees of my seminars and work sessions.

Get your plan into action and do something every day to reach your goals. If you have other obligations, be sure to prioritize your time to work on the promotion. Never let a day go by without doing some work on your project. Send out lots of information. Try new sources, be daring, and go for things that seem unattainable.

Make sure your letters of inquiry and other printed materials are grammatically sound and look professional. Send small samples. For example, if you are writing a cookbook, send a sample cookie and coffee, or a bookmark. Check local possibilities for talk shows, radio shows, hometown newspapers, and other publications. Cable TV is great, as there are so many family and craft and health shows (as well as other specialized programming) on the small cable stations.

You always want to reach as many potential customers as possible. The end result is sales. We are all salespeople before we are writers or inventors. Nothing happens until the product is sold. So have some fun, stick with it, and never give up—because you believe in yourself.

Public speaking is an important aspect of self-promotion. After all, as a self-promoter, you don't have anyone else to speak for you. Having the confidence that you are a competent public speaker will be very valuable in press conferences and interviews, and it can lead to a sideline that capitalizes on your expertise and, thus, promotes your products, as well. Vickie Sullivan tells us how to enhance any spoken presentation to make it a sure-fire vehicle for sales.

The Power of the Platform: Using Public Speaking to Create Credibility, Visibility, and Sales

By Vickie Sullivan

Imagine a group of potential clients in a room, hanging on your every word. They are already qualified, have expressed interest, and are intently listening. The media is in this room as well, taking pictures and furiously writing notes, quoting you. Is this a promoter's dream? No, just public speaking, one of the most effective tools to get visibility in a crowded market. The purpose of this piece is to give you a sense of why and how public speaking can create visibility, credibility, and yes, even more business.

Fortunately, there are plenty of opportunities to speak. According to the American Society of Association Executives, a typical association holds thirty-three meetings per year, and seventy-one percent will use speakers for their meetings. Industry studies indicate that associations alone spend $443 million for professional speakers every year. Combine both association events and corporate conferences, and you have over 100,000 opportunities every year to be visible. And the Number One source to fill these agendas? Experts such as yourself, who have products and services of interest to the audience.

Three Big Reasons

Why does public speaking create so much credibility and visibility? Three reasons: the invitation, the environment, and the audience.

The Invitation Why are you addressing a specific group? Because you were invited. And that invitation creates credibility long before you ever reach the podium. Once you've been invited, the marketing of your speech begins—by the group sponsoring you. Your host now has a vested interest in filling the room. They send fliers, alert the media, all on your behalf. The fact that someone, somewhere, thought your views were important enough to invite you to speak conveys credibility, even to those not coming to your speech. This is why it is very important to list your speaking schedule on your website, your newsletters, and even in networking.

The Environment All the publicity before the speech creates an environment set up for your success. As a guest speaker, you are like a visiting dignitary—your appearance is the focus of that meeting. Everyone wants you to feel welcome. You're the new person in the room, and people want to know more about you. Conversations before the meeting are geared toward your expertise, your views, and your background. In short, you're the star. Could there be a better environment for potential clients to check you out?

The Audience Unlike a sales situation, the audience enters the room with the belief that your message is credible. They believe that you have something interesting or substantial to say, otherwise, the host wouldn't have invited you to speak. Your message will be heard with an open mind rather than taken with a grain of salt. Not only does the audience have an open mind, they are also attracted to your topic, or they wouldn't be there. No one wastes time going to meetings that don't interest them. Qualified audiences (audiences that are already interested in your subject, product, or services) make speaking a very powerful sales tool.

Although speaking is a great visibility-building device, it is like any other tool—its effectiveness depends on how you use it. The two elements that make the difference between revenue-generating visibility and an exercise in futility are differentiation and leverage.

The Power of Differentiation

I knew a consultant, "Sam," who spoke in front of fifty potential customers at an association conference. He rehearsed and practiced every spare moment for weeks, and it showed. The applause was thunderous and a group gathered afterward, congratulating him on such a great presentation. Being a good networker, Sam gathered cards, took notes, and spent the next two weeks following up.

What happened during the follow-up phase shocked him. People who were so interested just a week ago barely remembered him. When they did remember the program, the willingness to discuss his services just wasn't there. For all his time and effort, Sam got applause and accolades, but no business. Has this ever happened to you? What's wrong with this picture?

Unfortunately, this scenario happens a lot. Many speakers believe that if their presentation skills are good enough, customers will come running to them after the speech. Speaking skills are important and great presentation skills will get you more speeches. But speaking skills alone won't move the audience to buy your services. Sam didn't do the most important thing that generates credibility and leads: differentiating the message.

What happens when an audience hears the same message over and over again? It becomes common knowledge. I call this "the dark side of abundance."

Here's what happens. When a message becomes abundant in the marketplace, the value of that message is diluted. What becomes diluted turns into a commodity, and commodities are selected by price rather than quality. Unless you are the cheapest source around, this downward spiral stops credibility and lead-generation cold.

Are you a commodity? Of course not! But that is what the audience believes if you repeat the same "universal truths" as your peers. Without a message that gives new insights, the audience sees you as just another Realtor, attorney, consultant, etc. who gave a good presentation. You know your material is too "abundant" if you hear the following feedback from your audience:

■ "Great refresher course."

■ "I already knew this, but it's great to hear it again."

■ "I've heard these points many times, but I like the way you explained them."

■ "Thanks for reminding me of what I already knew."

To prevent this, you must spend just as much time developing the message as you do rehearsing the speech. What is considered "differentiated" material?

When your message provides new information or a different take on what's already known, the audience perceives you differently, and your credibility soars. Below are three ways to create material that sets your expertise apart.

■ **Go narrow.** If the universal truths are already known, then why isn't everyone implementing them? Maybe because what isn't discussed are the distinctions, those little nuances that trip us up all the time. Where are those wrong turns located and why do we take them? Speakers that cover those areas are providing new material by delving deeper into the topic.

Key strategy: Assume that the audience agrees with your key points. Ask yourself, "What's keeping people from doing what I'm suggesting here?" Use your answer to develop new material and then spend the most time on that. Better yet, state the universal truth and use a story to illustrate the distinction.

- **Different applications.** Create great new material by using new applications for already known data. New tools that create major benefits will make you credible very quickly. Harvard Business School professor Jerry Zaltman does this by developing a way to use metaphors and pictures in market research to determine the real reason people buy products and services. Companies such as Nestle and Motorola have lined up to use this new process. Are these firms buying the results on how our brains use metaphors or the benefits of the application? Zaltman became a credible resource by applying what was already known in a different way.

Key strategy: Translate your ideas to a process and test the results. In your speeches, report the results and the process, as well as why it works.

- **From verbal to nonverbal.** Sometimes, what you don't say creates a lot of credibility. Platitudes and pontificating don't really show how much you know—audiences stop listening after a while anyway. Using stories, rhetorical questions, and other interactive processes will allow others to get your point without you telling them. This scenario sets up "The Power of Demonstration!" Audiences will give you credit for the insights they have during your presentation. You don't have to SAY the insight—they figure it out on their own and give you credit for it!

Key strategy: Focus on demonstrating your points instead of just telling the audience. Separate each point into two sections: "data dumps" and "now what?" The "data dumps" should focus on the distinctions, barriers, or the "big picture." The "now what?" uses exercises or rhetorical questions that makes the audience think about how they can use your knowledge.

Bottom line: Take your audience where they haven't gone before and they will take you to the bank.

Leverage

A differentiated message creates credibility—so now what? It's time to extend that credibility forward with leverage, the momentum that converts visibility into more opportunities and sales. Without momentum, a speech is just that—a speech. And your business is not making speeches, it's getting and keeping clients. Leverage extends the benefits and goodwill created from the speech and turns those benefits into opportunities. And opportunities to get more visibility, new clients, etc. are the reasons for giving the speech in the first place. Leverage occurs in two places: within the speech itself and around the event.

Within the Speech Although audiences come to you with an open mind, they also come in with perceptions that block leverage. Your speech must change those perceptions subtly without "pitching from the platform." (Making an obvious sales pitch is a major kiss of death—don't even *think* of doing this.) How? By making sure every point, every exercise, and every story, demonstrates three things:

1. That you can help them or their organization;
2. That your ideas work in their environment; and
3. That they need your help.

These three messages must be consistently demonstrated in the speech before you will plant the seed in the participants' minds that you can help them. The key here is consistent and subtle demonstration. Let's examine the above three messages in more depth.

Yes, you can help them. When I represented professional speakers, I would talk with participants after a speech to get my clients more business. After talking with thousands of audience members, the most common (and surprising) question was: "Does he/she speak to other groups?" Somehow the message that my client was a professional speaker did not register. The audience needs to learn that you have products and services without your selling them.

Key strategy: Your introduction is key here. Don't just say "consultant" or "coach." Mention how many people or organizations you have helped and in what way. Then, carry that idea forward by mentioning other audiences or clients in the context of your work. Example: "Of all the people I coach, there is one _____ that comes up every time..."

Yes, these ideas can work. Another very common comment from audience members is: "I loved the program, but I just don't see a fit." Translation: There's no connection between the material and their environment. Again, you can't tell the audience directly—participants also must get this second message on their own. When this happens, they are transformed into allies, on a personal mission to get you into their life or organization.

Key strategies: When customizing, ask your host about specific examples or instances and apply your message to them. That will switch the focus from teaching your material to applying it to their work environment. The audience will still learn, but they will also see the application. Also, use your clients (in their industry) as case studies. Be sure to make the client the star, not you.

Don't do this at home. Once a participant got really excited about my clients' services, a surprising thing happened: the audience member had just enough information to make him or her dangerous. Many people will believe that they have all the tools they need to implement your ideas. Keep in mind that many companies send people to conferences for a report on ideas/strategies to teach their co-workers. Audience members come in with the mind-set that asks, "What can I take from this program for this report?" If audiences believe they can do your work on their own, chances are your material was too abundant.

Key strategies: Telling stories that show the intricacies of your work will not only give more value, but will also point out the many pitfalls attendees need to know about. Experiential exercises are also great at showing all the pitfalls.

In short, leverage can't happen until the audience knows three things: your products and services are unique, you are effective in their environment, and they can't do it without you. Only then do the audience members start to think about taking the next step.

Creating Leverage Around the Event The audience is not the only place you can create leverage. The speech itself can be a vehicle to create many opportunities that extend your visibility. Again, speaking itself has credibility already built in. Use this to your advantage by leveraging before, during, and after the speech.

Before the speech, you have two major objectives: fill the room with qualified leads and create the most publicity around the event. Ideas include:

- Invite potential clients, media and "fans."
- Send a letter promoting the event to group mailing lists (key: focus on topic, not you or your services).
- Create rapport with "movers and shakers" with interviews for research.
- List the speech on your website, including details for registration.
- Many associations have "member news" sections in newsletters and journals; list the invitation there.

During the speech, you will be busy with networking and planting those seeds. Don't forget that you also want the contact information from audience members. But most importantly, you want to create "an invitation to call." In other words, you want the audience to give you permission to solicit them. Ideas include:

- Make sure you manage the audiences' perceptions (see earlier sections).

- Use audience members as examples, along with stories and quotes from your movers and shakers research.

- Offer to give away something (a special report works best here) for business cards.

- At the time you mention the special report, say something like "If you want additional information about me or my company, just put an "*" on your card and we'll take care of that, too."

Best time to do this: after break and during Q & A

Worst time to do this: before break and after opening

Aftermath: More Work

After the speech, you'll want to bask in your glory—but don't. You still have work to do. Your objectives in this phase are to continue the interest and to convert interest into sales or more opportunities for visibility. Ideas include:

- Send a thank-you letter to the participants—your audience will be shocked!

- Create a "next step" in your promotional effort by offering participants a discount on your normal fees.

- Promote long-term relationships with movers and shakers by keeping in touch.

- Follow up on "*" cards with two key questions: "Do you want information for your files or do you want to explore with me how to use my services in your specific situation?" If they say "both" to your question, then ask "What is the timeline for you to decide to move forward?"

Public speaking can be one of the most effective tools in your publicity toolbox. Use it wisely, and create more opportunities than you can ever imagine. Good luck, and I'll see you on the circuit!

chapter **2**

Print Media

The print media—newspapers and magazines—are the most traditional tools in building a publicity campaign. Salvatore Caputo, a veteran newspaper journalist, discusses how to get around the major obstacles that can stop your pitch from getting newspaper coverage.

Getting Ink in Newspapers

By Salvatore Caputo

I spent many of my 21 years in the newspaper business as the target of publicity pitches. Some worked and got ink in the paper. The vast majority didn't. Why?

Many publicity people, neophyte self-promoters and seasoned public relations professionals alike, showed little or no understanding of the mechanics that drove our coverage. They seemed bent on a vicious deforestation campaign, wasting paper in a hopeless shotgun publicity approach: spray every moving target and you're bound to hit something!

That's not a formula for success. Many reporters and editors have thrown out piles of unsolicited publicity pitches without even opening the envelopes because one look at the return address told them the pitch would be inappropriate.

Your goal is to get these news professionals to at least open your envelope, and that means clearly defining your goals. Why are you pitching to this particular newspaper? Where does potential publicity from this newspaper fit into your plans? Who at this newspaper would be most receptive to your pitch? When you can answer each of these questions in a simple sentence, then it's time to make your move.

Space is Precious

When making a pitch, remember that editors and reporters aren't committed to you, but to their readers. They want to bring useful and interesting information and stories to their audience. Your job is to persuade them that their readers are your target audience, and that what you're selling will be of interest to those readers.

This is crucial because of the space limitations of newspapers. I watched our book-review editor tear her hair out as she attempted to decide which books would make the cut for the limited space that we had to devote to them.

Our paper published three to four full-size book reviews on one Sunday newspaper page. Simple math tells us that if 50,000 books are published each year, we reviewed a meager percentage of them. For the most part, we did not even have a staff reviewer. Staffers, me included, contributed reviews on an occasional basis, but most of the reviews came from other newspapers through our wire services.

Another two columns of space featured mini-reviews of another dozen or so books, but that didn't mine that mountain of books very deeply either. In one of our weekday editions, there was an occasional column reviewing children's books. Blurbs about health books appeared in the weekly health section. The garden writer would make a rare mention of a few gardening books, and other specialists who covered travel, sports, business, art, and music (among others) also would look at books that fit into their beats. (All of these specialists represent targets for pitches, if your book or other product fits into one of their realms.)

With so little space, the emphasis was on books that we thought would appeal to a cross section of readers. That meant things we thought would be "sure things" or as close as we could get to them. Things that, in a lot of ways, didn't *need* publicity. Tom

Clancy? Stephen King? Sure! And any big celebrity book that came along. You'll be competing against those guys just as hard for newspaper space as you will for shelf space in the bookstores, because most editors will try to mentally gauge the amount of buzz that will surround each book. The biggest buzz gets the biggest play, or presentation, in the newspaper.

This doesn't mean we didn't publish reviews of books by first-time authors, but they were few and quite often came from a major book publisher. The major publishers don't like to make risky moves. They carefully choose projects that they believe will give them a good return on their investment. To us at the newspaper, that guaranteed that there'd be at least some initial interest in each project they put out. Even a book that was lambasted by the reviewer would be something that people wanted to read about, because they'd already heard about it.

Even so, all the major publishers' projects didn't get covered in the paper.

This is a major daily newspaper with a growing circulation. The Sunday paper routinely tops 600,000 circulation. If it's so tight on space for books, what chance does a self-promoting book author or publisher have?

Prepare for Success

Sure, you need to have thick skin and be prepared for rejection. However, the situation is far from hopeless. Remember that reviews and book pages are only the most obvious way to publicize your book. For instance, you can almost always get calendar listings for speaking engagements or book-signings that arise from your book (again, on a space-available basis, but generally speaking, because calendar items are short, the space is available more often than not).

The right preparation will help maximize the chances of getting ink in a newspaper. Remember that newspaper editors are busy,

busy, busy. You can attribute part of this to disorganization if you'd like, but the major culprit is the corporate determination to improve the productivity of every employee. Our book editor didn't just handle books. She edited the movie section, television section, and other entertainment coverage. Books, however important they might have been to her personally, had to be handled efficiently and as effortlessly as possible.

Keep that in mind when planning your publicity effort. Get to the point quickly in press releases. Put the most important information—title, author's name, publication date—near the top of press releases, and make sure every piece of paper (and any photos and cover reproductions) has your name and contact information on it. Doing so will make it that much easier for the editor to find the information when the time comes.

When you do your follow-up calls on your mailings (editors will hate me for saying this, but you *must* do follow-up calls or you'll never know if the appropriate person even got your mailing), approach editors politely in a businesslike fashion. Rehearse your follow-up calls before you make them. Keep them short and to the point, but don't be a robot. It's OK to have a personality, and the editor will appreciate it as long as you don't waste time. Always ask whether the editor is on deadline.

After you've made your pitch, if they say "no" firmly, don't push. Just thank them for their time and say, "Good-bye." If they seem less than firm, you can try to engage them in more conversation to find out whether it's a firm "no" or a "maybe." Many editors feel guilty turning you down if your story is even remotely newsworthy.

Be persistent, but don't be pesky. Try to get a firm commitment of when you should call back to make any subsequent follow-up calls. Then, be sure to call at that time. If another follow-up call is necessary, wait at least five working days before calling again (unless you've got a very timely angle that needs to be worked more quickly—such as an impending press conference).

Big Angles for Big Papers

Don't approach a metropolitan daily immediately, unless you live in the newspaper's coverage area and can exploit the hometown angle. If you can get a clipping from a major daily in your hometown, that's very useful in building credibility and allows you to skip some steps in the plan I'm about to outline.

A major daily will not buy the hometown angle alone. It has to be coupled with some other distinguishing factor. Is this book timely? Don't publish a guide to vacationing in Phoenix just as winter's ending, for instance, unless the guide is specifically pointed at the idea that summer's a great time to be in the city. Is this book the first of its kind? Is the author a distinguished expert in this field? Does the book tell the untold story of some sensational event? Is there a great story behind the book?

One angle that will usually earn some coverage is if your book has sold surprisingly well. If it has, approach the business department of your local newspaper or a local business newspaper. They love to run stories that feature surprising sales numbers. Why is this a story? Because most first books don't sell at all.

Climbing the Ladder

The best way to approach a major daily is to work up the ladder of newspapers in your publicity campaign. The lowest rung is the weekly or biweekly community newspaper. Some of these are free "shoppers" that are thrown on your driveway, more advertisement than news. Send a press release to your local shopper, and they'll most likely be happy to have another item from the community to fill the space around the ads. Your press release might be reprinted verbatim or with a few minor changes. However, it's also possible that the shopper will be so intrigued that they'll assign an article on your book. If so, clip the story and put it in your media kit.

Next, you might hit the higher-level weeklies. These are publications that people buy—through a subscription or at a newsstand.

Include good clips from the shoppers in your press kit. Don't include any verbatim reprints of press releases. However gratifying they are to you, the editor will see that your press release and the clipping are one and the same, and you will have built no credibility, which is your only goal at this point.

Again, if this tier of newspapers responds, take the good clippings from these and go to the small-market dailies. By the time you've got some clippings from these smaller publications, you'll have gained experience in what approaches work and don't work with newspaper editors. Now, you're ready to try your newly honed publicity skills on the big boys.

The big boys come in three classes. The biggest of the big in circulation and influence are *The New York Times, Wall Street Journal, Washington Post, Los Angeles Times,* and *USA Today.* When approaching these markets, know what they're about. They are so few, that you should take the time to read through a few issues at a library. Where do you see your book fitting in? Do you need to refocus your press release to get them interested? It's worth the effort, because clippings from these newspapers impart a great deal of credibility to your campaign. You won't sell millions of books, but you can bet the bookstores and distributors will note the coverage you're getting there, especially if you send them clippings.

The rung just below would be newspapers in the long-established Eastern seaboard, Midwestern and major Texas markets—Boston, Chicago, St. Louis, Miami, Philadelphia, Kansas City, Dallas and the like.

Next would be the major markets in the West—Denver, Phoenix, Seattle, San Francisco and others.

I would start with that third tier and move eastward, adding clips from each tier to the batch going to the next tier.

The clippings aren't meant to impress jaded media members. Rather, they're meant to show that other people took you seriously and that you have a track record. Few writers or editors want to go out on a limb for a complete unknown, but once you develop a track record, they warm up a bit. One warning, this psychology works best when you're dealing with media that are at nearly the same level. If you send a clipping from a small-town newspaper to the editor at the *New York Times Book Review* section, it's unlikely to help your cause much, unless it's also accompanied by clips from higher rungs on the newspaper ladder.

Finding the Papers

A good source for developing your newspaper media list is *Editor & Publisher* magazine's annual guide to newspapers. *Editor & Publisher* is a newspaper trade magazine, and its guide lists newspapers state by state. This format gives you a rough picture of each newspaper's clout in the state, something that won't be as readily apparent in *Bacon's Media Directory*, although that publication does list circulation of each newspaper, too. Many libraries have copies of both or other similar publications that list newspapers, their markets, and their editors.

Don't be discouraged. A good story that fits the newspaper's readers will get you in. Be brutally honest with yourself and make sure you have a good story before you make the approach.

Having sat on both sides of the editor's desk at magazines and newspapers, Sarah Eden Wallace stresses the importance of making your publicity materials "editor friendly."

Publicity That Speaks Volumes

By Sarah Eden Wallace

When it comes to getting publicity in a newspaper or magazine, think about cooking: when bone-tired worker bees come home from a tough day at the office, do they want to check recipes, call Cousin Eunice for that secret ingredient they can't remember, chop, stir and simmer? Or will they opt for the convenient jar sauce in a delightful package that promises a healthy balanced meal in fifteen minutes?

Jar sauce, naturally.

This is where your perfectly prepared publicity materials come in. In the pressure-cooker of the newsroom environment, your taste-tested press kit is the jar sauce: a well-seasoned, nicely packaged instant mix that makes putting together a story a cinch—and lands you coverage pronto.

Read on for the recipe for a publicity campaign that gets you cooking on the front burner, instead of settling for cold leftovers.

Think Like an Editor

Having worked in daily and magazine journalism for almost fifteen years, I'll give you the straight-from-the-newsroom view on the likeliest ways to get placement. Throughout this chapter I've included "Insider Tips," "Dos and Don'ts," and translations of *journalese* (newsroom lingo) to help you understand an editor's outlook.

First and foremost, timing is everything when it comes to getting coverage. Know your target publications' deadlines. You could have the greatest story idea in the galaxy, but if the book has already gone to bed (journalese: the paper or magazine has already been laid out and sent to the printer), you're toast.

Monthly magazines need material months, if not half a year, in advance. Daily or weekly newspapers are more flexible, but still plan on sending your materials weeks ahead. Media directories (available at your local library), like the *Writer's Market*, often list production schedules. When in doubt, mail four months in advance and then resend if necessary.

Insider Tip

Read the magazine. Familiarize yourself with the kinds of stories they run and angle your press materials along those lines. Are they family-oriented ("Lawyer dad offers advice on surviving divorce") or geared to hard-news angles ("Study shows dads' income drops after divorce"). Customize your news releases to match the tone of your target publication.

Now, visualize what's going on in a newsroom. Keyboards are clattering; phones are ringing at desks heaped with papers, Post-its and books; and if deadlines are coming up (one reporter friend of mine calls them "dreadlines"), people are in a coffee and candy bar-fueled frenzy.

In this scenario, the likelihood of your story being picked up is directly proportional to how easy you make it for the editor to glean a story from your materials. A well-organized press kit with clean copy and strong visuals that lets a busy reporter whip up a story in 15 minutes is your goal.

Keep this in mind when you put together your press kit: give the reporter/editor all the information they need to potentially write a story without ever having seen your book or talked to you. Although they might call for an interview, always assume you have to send enough information so they can write it on a desert island, if needed.

The Making of a Press Kit

- The most important feature: artwork of your book.

  A picture is literally worth a thousand words. In this era of the MTV mind-set, publication layouts often devote more space to pictures than print. It is quite common for a story to run solely because there were good visuals or graphics that came with the story. If you provide quality artwork, it saves the editor from having to generate an assignment for the art department.

  If you're not including a review copy of the book, enclose a blad (sample book cover) or high-quality 35mm color slide or black-and-white photo of the book. It can be a good idea to add a black-and-white photo and 35mm color slide of the author (send both because production requirements vary from one publication to another).

  All photography must be of professional quality. Snapshots are absolutely out of the question—a sure-fire sign of an amateur operation—and could earn you a quick trip to the wastebasket.

- A half-page or one-page biography of the author and a brief write-up of the book—no more than two pages.

  Any news story is built based on the Five Ws and an H: Who, What, Where, When, Why, and How. So base your write-up on that format. Again, make it as easy as possible for the reporter.

  The Ws should be included in your lead paragraph. Also, think of a clever lead, or mention why your book is significant: anything that's first, biggest, longest, exclusive, different ("the first look at divorce from the dad's point of view").

Insider Tip

Reporters on "dreadline" often borrow liberally from news releases. It's not anybody's idea of great journalism, but sometimes you'll see news releases run verbatim. The more you write your news release like a newspaper story, the more likely passages will be lifted straight out.

- Basics that your news release should include are a condensed profile of the author, the name of the publisher, when the book will be released, where else it's been reviewed or some sense of reader response to the book.

  Be sure to include when it's available (the publication date), where it is available (any 800 numbers, bookstores, or websites), and how to order it: the price and any ordering information.

  Reporters are usually glad to run an 800-number or list a website because we don't want readers calling up and clogging our voice mail with questions on how to order the book.

- Your business card. A high-dollar but effective method is to send out Rolodex cards with your name and info preprinted on it.

- Always triple-check your spelling. It must be impeccable, or you lose credibility and look like an amateur.

- The best tip I can give you (besides sending material well before deadlines and checking your spelling) is to localize if possible.

  The mantra of today's newspaper is "localize, localize, localize." A publication is umpteen times more likely to write about you if there's a local angle: the author went to college in that town; the author grew up in that town; someone from that town is featured in the book: the author is from the same state; the author went to college in the state. (Once I reviewed a book just because one of the characters is looking for her AWOL husband in Tucson.) Any editor's ears will perk up when they hear a local angle—make sure to mention it in your phone follow-up.

Advanced Dos and Don'ts

Do use AP style[1] (journalese: a set of grammar and spelling rules outlined in the *Associated Press Stylebook*) when writing your materials. Most bookstores can order the stylebook for you, or most college bookstores carry it. Know the language, use the style, smooth the way for the reporter.

Do include graphics or factoids Newspaper and magazine editors know that readers raised on Nintendo and thirty-second commercials have the attention span of fleas on Ritalin, so they are always looking for quick, vivid ways to convey information or a story. I had an editor who always asked whether we could "graphisize a story." It may not have been grammatical, but she knew the picture-book approach to news reporting worked with readers.

What this means to you is to include material that can be easily "graphisized"—bulleted lists of information tidbits (such as "Top ten reasons men divorce" or "Pickup lines that work with divorced men"). One Phoenix company that publishes corporate training materials sent out a humorous list, a la David Letterman, of "Top Ten Ways to Avoid a Sexual Harassment Suit After the Office Christmas Party." It was picked up by newspapers across the country, including the *Wall Street Journal*. If they use the tidbits, the publication will usually attribute them to a source. If it's your book, bingo, there's your book title in newspapers across the country.

---

[1] AP style is generally followed within the newspaper industry. However, many magazine and book publishers follow the Chicago Manual of Style, so a working knowledge of both helps. *LFR*

Do use review copies strategically I know most publicity experts suggest sending tons of review copies. But as often as not, these end up in newsroom corners in towering stacks that are later sold off in a charity fund-raiser for the local homeless shelter. So don't assume sending a review copy means you'll be covered.

By all means, send out review copies, but you might consider sending them to your top 100 or 200 prospects. For prospects lower on your list, include a form in your press kit that lets reporters make a simple fax request for a review copy if they want one. Then you'll know you've got well-qualified prospects, plus you've captured information about them—and built a pre-qualified mailing list for future promotions.

Exterior Decorating: The Outside of a Press Kit

One of the best book-publicity packages I ever saw consisted of a clear plastic 6-by-9-inch envelope. The blad, or book cover, had been inserted into the package with the news release, slides, and other information folded inside. The cover, which showed through the clear plastic, made an eye-catching, attractive envelope that stood out from the rest of the two-foot heap of mail on my desk. It was a clever presentation that instantly conveyed that this was an appealing, professionally handled book that merited further investigation—and the intriguing packaging invited further scrutiny. That is exactly what you want your outside packaging to do.

Insider Tip

Newsrooms are bombarded with paper. Think of the junk mail you get at home, magnify it a thousandfold, and add in faxes and e-mail. One food editor at a major daily has a desk that looks like Hurricane Mitch does her housekeeping (though she could find any cookbook in seconds). Whatever you send to the newspaper has to stand out from that kind of information overload.

Dos and Don'ts

If you can't afford a custom, professionally designed folder like most PR companies use, one economical approach is to design a great-looking mailing label with your logo and then use that on the outside of store-bought folders.

Use humor. If apropos, try gimmicks: attach a penny ("penny-saving ideas for home repair") or an aspirin caplet (a "cure" for holiday headaches) to your news release (make sure your gimmick won't spill and smear on your materials).

Design a visual on the cover to entice the reporter into opening your press kit. Nothing on the cover makes it look like there's not much inside.

Though it's not essential, it's a nice touch if you personalize your mailing. With the mail-merge programs that computers offer, it's easy enough to do.

A good way to find these names is in media directories, such as the *Hudson's* directory, at your local library. Or you can buy mailing lists like *Publicity Blitz Media on Disk Directory* (800-784-4359), about $300 for 19,000 contacts.

Don't go too slick. Sink your money into good-quality phone follow-up with the media, not a slick, four-color, razzle-dazzle press kit. You can put together a solid, professional press kit using the tips above.

On the other hand, don't go tacky. Don't send fuzzy, blurry news releases that look like they were mimeographed on the school copier. Keep your materials clean, crisp and clear.

Don't use those dime-store school-report folders. They just shriek "amateur."

Insider Tip

Diversify. Most newshounds are great at foisting their mail off on colleagues and will pass on books and news releases to someone they think might use them. But you should strategize along those same lines, too. See if there's another angle—send a sports book to the sports editor, not just the book reviewer. Send a cooking book to food editors, fashion book to fashion reporters, child-rearing or self-help books to lifestyle or features sections.

Persistence—Not Pestering—Pays Off

Here's what can separate you from an above-the-fold story and the wastebasket: Follow-up.

Do keep it short—reporters are rushed. Practice your pitch, and use the same structure as the news release. Work up a script that tells Who, What, Where, When, Why and How in thirty seconds.

If you have to leave a voice-mail message, KISS: Keep It Short and Simple. Nothing makes a reporter on deadline fume more than a rambling waste of time.

Do repeat your name and number at the end of the message. The reporter will be listening throughout your spiel and then decide if he or she wants to call you back. This way, they don't have to replay the message to catch your numbers.

Do mention any local angles or other angles (the author will be appearing in your area, the book just won an award, the author is speaking at a local university) up front. Don't bury your lead, as they say in j-school. (journalese: Start with your strongest point, as they teach you in journalism school).

Don't nag. Call once, then follow up in a week or so. When reporters are on deadline with a major story, they may not even look at their mail or check voice-mail for days, and then nothing is as irritating as a flack (journalese: a bothersome public-relations account executive) loading up voice-mail with long questions about "when are you going to do a story about so-and-so?" Remember, the reporter is probably getting dozens of calls a day.

Do simply ask, "Did you get the material I sent you about Susie Smith and her new book? I would be glad to provide photos or art-work if you need it, or arrange an interview with the author."

Do make sure you respond as soon as possible if a reporter does call you back. If a reporter's on deadline, they need an answer within an hour or at the very least that day. Leave instructions with your front office to page you; in your voice-mail, mention cell-phone or pager numbers or an alternate person who can help.

Positive Postscripts

If your book is covered in a publication, stay in touch. Thank yous are nice. Send a card or write a note on your next release, thanking them for the story. I always appreciated hearing how a story or review affected book sales.

Once you have that connection with a reporter or editor, cultivate it. Send them newsworthy updates. Mention the previous story in any correspondence you have with them or in any forthcoming publicity materials.

Now that you've got an insider's look at how to get coverage in print, here's the kicker (journalese: wrap-up of a story). As the book *Running a One-Person Business* says, anything you do to market your product will be successful. Likewise, anything you do to gain publicity will be successful. So get to work—you've got deadlines to meet!

We all strive to get our books and products reviewed in just about any publication. We always hope they'll be positive, but even when they're not, we comfort ourselves with the notion that ANY mention is better than no mention. After all, the survival of our books or products demands visibility. So what's the inside story on book reviews? I can't think of anyone to better answer that question than accomplished book reviewer William D. Bushnell.

Book Reviews: You Can't Live Without Them

By William D. Bushnell

Asking an author what he thinks about book reviewers is like asking a fire hydrant how it feels about dogs. However, as an author burdened with the promotion of your own book, you cannot escape the fact that book reviewers are essential to your marketing efforts.

Reviews sell books. They are cheaper than advertising and it should be no surprise that readers believe in them more.

Depending on the publication, book reviews can reach a widespread audience or they can target a specific region or a market niche.

More than 40,000 new books are published in this country every year, and yours is just one of them. Competition for review space is great, so it is important that you understand the book-review game, how editors select books for review, where to send your review copies, how to use the Internet for reviews, pitfalls to avoid, and even whether you should hire your own reviewer to help promote your book.

Fear of Reviewers

Now is a good time to acknowledge that most writers are wary of, nay fear, reviewers. For some authors, the fear is justified. Their work deserves to get creamed and they usually know it. For most, however, the fear is unreasonable—the fear of the Bogeyman of the Bad Review. Author Thomas Fleming expresses it best: "Whether written by fellow writers or professional reviewers, the all-out assault is what every writer dreads. I have heard it described in various ways—snide, dismissive, insulting. Let us call it, for the sake of hyperbole, the ground-zero review. In it, the writer is often urged to seek another line of work."

Well, it is seldom that bad, and who knows, you might even get a favorable review. No matter what, even a bad review is better than no review at all, because after all, nobody will ever buy your book unless they know about it. And, believe it or not, it is better to be embarrassed than to be ignored. Of course, having a thick skin is helpful, too.

Most magazines and newspapers print book reviews, and there are a number of magazines that publish nothing but reviews. Magazines with large book review sections include *Booklist, Publishers Weekly, Library Journal, Independent Publisher, Bloomsbury Review,* and *The Women's Review of Books,* among many others.

Some of the larger and more prestigious periodicals will use their own staff for review work, while most others will use a stable of freelance reviewers. Either way, it is the editor who decides what books will get the coveted column inches of space each week.

Know the Review Markets

Editors receive heaps of books every month, all with hopeful cover letters pleading for review. Many books are uncorrected proof copies sent months in advance of publication, others are the smooth copy ready for sale. The publication's house rules will usually determine which books will be considered for review and which will be eliminated. For example, the *Washington Post Book World* is not interested in how-to, self-help, or very technical books. Selection criteria vary greatly, but are normally based on a balance of expediency, reader interests, timeliness, and space, rather than a snooty sense of elitism.

In your pursuit of a review, your first task will be to amass a pile of review copies of your book. Next, do some research into the review market for your book's subject and audience. If your book is about trout fishing, do not waste your time, money, and a review copy by sending a book to *Car and Driver*. *Ulrich's International Periodical Directory* is an excellent resource for researching all the magazines and newspapers that pertain to your book's subject or locale. It is arranged by subject and geographic area and provides all the contact information you will need to send review copies to the publications you select. You will find it at the reference desk of your local public library. And think BIG. Go beyond the local weekly newspaper and pursue regional and national publications, too.

Contacting Editors

A brief, businesslike, straightforward cover letter should accompany each review copy, addressed to the editor personally. Tell the editor exactly what you want, but avoid the fanciful and too-cute approach. Once your review copy hits the editor's desk, stay out of it. Do not badger the editor, or your book will most likely end up in the dumpster. The editor will make the decision, and you might be fortunate enough to get a review. Naturally, the more review copies you send out, the greater the chance that your book will be selected for review somewhere. Most editors will prefer to review books published in the last twelve months, so you cannot wait too long to get started. Your window of review opportunity closes a little more with each passing month.

Internet Opportunities

Another source for you to exploit for book reviews comes through the unregulated, wide-open electronic medium of the Internet. As intimidating as it might seem, the Internet has the potential to attract a larger reading audience than print magazines and newspapers ever dreamed. Review magazines like *Publishers Weekly* and *The Hungry Mind Review* have already tapped into cyberspace and more will follow. With the click of a mouse, Amazon.com, encourages readers to submit reviews.

The Internet is filled with sites for online book review opportunities, like *The Edge City Review, History Review On-Line,* and the *Electronic Library.* You will have to do some cyber legwork to uncover submission requirements for your review copies, but the results could be well worth the effort. All online sites have an e-mail address for you to query directly regarding your review copy submission. The only difficulty you may have will be determining which are reputable review sites and which are the fly-by-night sites nobody cares about. Since this forum is so new, is unregulated, and is growing so quickly, your judgment will be your only guide.

Hiring a Reviewer?

With your review copies in the mail and your patience wearing thin, you may be tempted to give yourself a boost by hiring your own reviewer to help promote your book. This practice is not normally followed, for when you hire a reviewer, the reviewer ceases to be an independent, objective critic and instead becomes a publicist, your employee. Some writers, however, would prefer a favorable review to an honest one, but there are risks. Your hired reviewer may not like your book. Are you then going to pay for an unflattering review? You will if you are smart. You do not want to make enemies, and besides, the reviewer may review another book of yours in the future. And if the review is positive, you won't know whether the reviewer means it, or feels obligated to like it because of the paycheck. You will always wonder.

If you continue with your own reviewer, have a clear plan for what you hope to accomplish. Professional reviewers will have many contacts and can advise you on where the review should be submitted. Only one review may be submitted at a time to any one publication, and there is no guarantee an unsolicited review (one not assigned by an editor) will be published despite the reviewer's credentials. Still, this type of review promotion does work occasionally, but it will cost you some money. A hired reviewer will want to be paid upfront, whether the review is published or not.

Use Reviews in Your Marketing

Once reviews have appeared in print they can still contribute to your marketing effort. Make good, clear copies of the best reviews (the most favorable, of course!) and use them in your press kits. You can also include copies of reviews with your cover letter when you send out additional review copies to other publications. Seeing that a book has already received positive attention elsewhere, an editor may be more inclined to consider it for a review before his direct competition gets it. Even book reviews can be scooped!

Since you are already hustling your own book in pursuit of recognition, sales, and income, do not overlook the value of book reviews in your plan. Magazines, newspapers, and the Internet can all provide an outlet for reviews of your book, but you will still have to work for it. You cannot depend on luck, for luck is an unexpected bonus. You can, however, depend on a solid, well-researched plan, and a lot of review copies sent to the right people in a timely fashion. Your patience and perseverance will pay off and you will soon see reviews of your book in print. And won't that be nice?

When seeking promotional opportunities, it's good to think "outside the box." Marketing expert Alf Nucifora discusses the many benefits he reaps by offering his expertise in a free column that is now carried by more than forty newspapers. He gains far more by giving his advice away than you would think.

You Too Can Be a Columnist

By Alf Nucifora

In 1996, I was approached by the publisher of the *Atlanta Business Chronicle*, the city's leading weekly business newspaper, to write a marketing column geared toward small business. This 1,000-word, fortnightly piece was to be an informational, how-to marketing guide that would help simplify and clarify the confusing and sometimes intimidating world of marketing.

Today, the article runs in more than 50 business publications around the United States, including weekly newspapers, frequent-flier magazines and trade publications. It has garnered a cult audience of more than a million weekly readers from both small business and the Fortune 500 corporate world.

From One to Many

At first, the intention was simply to write a column that was specific and relevant to the Atlanta marketplace. However, because the *Atlanta Business Chronicle* is one of forty similar publications in the American City Business Journal (ACBJ) family, other editors took note of the column and picked it up for their own use.

For those that didn't, a letter was sent out every ninety days announcing the column's availability, together with an offer to customize it and/or help promote via in-market guest speeches and seminars. As a result of this marketing effort, the column has now been syndicated to all ACBJ publications. The relationship with the editors of these publications is now so strong that I am routinely requested to address ACBJ editorial, marketing, and corporate staff on the fundamentals of newspaper marketing.

It's Not Just Another Freebie

I've elected not to seek a fee from any legitimate publication that wants to run the column. I already maintain a lucrative consulting and seminar practice and, as such, the dollars that would be generated by the column would be purely incidental. In a tight business-publishing marketplace where most guest and freelance writers are paid a mere pittance, why risk not being picked up by another publication because of a few incidental dollars?

What do I get in return? A lot, including high visibility in the nation's leading chain of weekly business publications; marketing authority status; a significant number of leads for my paid speech and seminar practice; continual requests for paid consulting advice; and 10,000 to 15,000 e-mail responses each year, including feedback on the column and requests for additional information. Every e-mail correspondent is added to a growing database, which I use for my marketing efforts, such as promoting my new book, *The Best of Shoestring Marketing*. In addition, these same readers were offered the opportunity to subscribe to a free, monthly online newsletter that kicked off in January 2000.

Many Benefits

Is it worth the time and effort?

As trite as it might seem, I get the satisfaction of being able to provide marketing help to people who want it, need it, and appreciate it. That can mean more than the business opportunity and the glory.

From the start, the Shoestring Marketing Column was viewed not as a revenue generator, but as brand support. The brand in question is "Nucifora." That's ultimately what generates the dollars. But, as in the case of any successful brand, from Coca-Cola to McKinsey, there must be an on-going and consistent effort to solidify the brand name and keep it prominent in the eyes of the public. What better way to accomplish this objective than to have a column featured in respected business publications, on a continuing basis, where the author's expertise is clearly evident and accentuated?

One of the offshoots of this publishing effort is that I often am approached by other publications for permission to reprint the columns. These run the gamut from industry trade publications to airline magazines. The most satisfying of all are the requests from corporate marketing and training departments to have the columns reprinted for in-house use. A prime example is the request from Five Star Publications to be featured in this very book.

An attendant benefit of writing a regular column is the necessity to be constantly seeking new story ideas and maintaining an up-to-date knowledge base of trend information and applications practice. In the fast-moving world of marketing, I have to constantly remind myself to be out in front of where the marketplace is heading. As an example, I made a concerted effort to learn about the Internet and its implications for marketing in the new millennium before it exploded. In the late 1980s, I was recognized as one of the premier instructors on the subject of database marketing, which is only now beginning to achieve critical-mass acceptance. A regular column keeps you sharp, alert, and always a step ahead. If you're not, your readers will quickly let you know. They become non-readers.

It's important to appreciate the value of the ripple effect that a published column can generate, and the necessity to capitalize on that effect. For instance, in promoting my new book, I considered it vital to track every reader response and be prepared to send an e-mail or snail-mail announcement as soon as the book was released. Every letter or inquiry from a reader got a personalized response within five working days. Naturally, I also asked each of the publications on my roster to review the book and give me as much publicity support as possible. In asking for that support, I show the editors and publishers that my column is working, that their readers appreciate it and that they want to see and hear more from me. And I have the stats to prove it, since I keep a running record of reader responses by column and by publication.

The Value of a Website

Let me also stress the value of a website. Everything I publish and print is always sealed with fax number, e-mail, and Web address. The website particularly is the repository of everything that anyone would ever want to know about the Nucifora brand: consulting, speeches, background information, article archives, etc. The key is to always provide the reader with the opportunity to get more information and contact Alf Nucifora if the occasion demands. That's what building a brand is all about.

Asking for the Order

I was lucky enough to be approached by a publication based on my marketing reputation. What happens if you're the one making the approach? It's not really all that difficult. Assuming you have the knowledge base and the writing skills, the rest is nothing more than desire, confidence, and a willingness to ask. The print media are always looking for good writers with a fresh perspective and especially those who will do it for free.

Call the publisher or the editor and pitch your idea. Always support the pitch with sample writing or a spec presentation. Emphasize what the benefit will be for the publication, for example, covering new territory, unique writing style, a different slant, scooping the competition, etc. It can work and it did in my case, when I pitched a program idea to Atlanta's leading radio station and secured a five-nights-a-week, three-hour talk-radio program in prime time without any inside contacts.

You might also want to contact a publication's current columnists to find out how they did it. I've referred five other budding columnists to the Atlanta Business Chronicle. In every case, it was a matter of serendipity. The newspaper needed a writer for a new subject area and sought my advice about who the experts around town were. I was happy to provide the recommendation.

chapter 3

Broadcast
Media

Radio and television can have a major impact on your publicity efforts. Being on a low budget is no reason to exclude them from your marketing plan. Explaining how to get your message onto broadcast and cable TV is Jess Todtfeld, an assistant producer at the Fox News Channel, Fox's 24-hour cable network.

How to Get Free Publicity on Television

By Jess Todtfeld

No one will argue if you say that television is a medium that exerts a powerful influence on people. Everyone knows that advertising financially supports the shows that we see on television. Advertisers are not stupid; they wouldn't pay the big bucks if they didn't know that their ads have the power to influence millions of people. The message that comes through the television is stronger than any message from billboards, magazines, radio, or any other medium. This is why you want your message to be on television. The question remains, "How do I get television producers, the people between me and those cameras, to help me out?"

Don't Worry, Be Happy!

The first step is to acquire the right mind-set. By the right mind-set, I mean you should put away any anxieties you may have. Instead, use that energy to become excited about this new challenge and potential opportunity. Many people I have spoken to get worried about this process. It is not as difficult as one might think.

Some get nervous at the prospect of calling up a busy producer to bother him/her about whatever it is that they are trying to publicize. To ease the anxiety that might be associated with this, I will tell you a few secrets that will make this seemingly arduous process a breeze. Hey, you have made it this far. You have something to promote. Not many people can say they had anything worthwhile to say or promote on television, so you should be proud of your accomplishment. Now it's time to take that accomplishment (and the newfound confidence that comes with it), transfer it to the most exciting medium there is, and get the results you are looking to achieve.

First off, the job of a TV producer is to come up with interesting ideas that they think viewers might want to see. Part of their job is hunting down these ideas so that their bosses think they are doing a good job. Your call is most likely helping them do their job. What you have to do is pitch your idea for a segment on their show. You might think it strange to use a word like pitching in this circumstance. Usually we associate pitching with the creative process, for example, the script for a new movie or sitcom. But really, television news programs and talk shows work the same way. There are thousands of ideas for segments or shows. With so many to choose from or to research, producers want to select only those they think will make for interesting television. If you can make your pitch a persuasive one, you have just made this person's life a little bit easier. The more work you can do for producers through all parts of the process, the more it will benefit you in the long run.

Second, you would be surprised at how young many of today's television producers are. Why am I telling you this? It can be calming to know that many of the professionals on the other end of the phone are half your age. It may give you the confidence you need to explain to them why their viewers would benefit from a segment done on you, your book, or your product.

And third, if you don't do it, no one will. It's better to try and fail than not to have tried at all. You can do nothing and get no publicity—so take your best shot.

I'll Scratch Your Back, If You'll Scratch Mine!

Let's say that you are trying to publicize a book that you have written. Let's say that the topic is needlepoint. What you really want is to get the word out about your book so that people will buy it. The television producer wants interesting programming, so the question becomes, "How can everyone be happy and get what they want?"

Simple. Put yourself in the shoes of the other person. If you were the producer of say, a local morning talk show, would you put an author on television whose pitch is "I want everyone to know that I have a new book about needlepoint"? No. Right off, it sounds boring. If you were the producer, you would want to find the most interesting topic for your show. It's your job as your own publicist to convince the producer that you are the ticket to interesting television, so be more creative in pitching your idea. A better pitch might be: "How about a segment on a stress-reducing pastime that more Americans are discovering every day?" Or you could try, "What is it about needlepoint that is attracting Generation X?" Already the producer's brain can start to envision how this segment will develop into something that the average viewer will stay tuned to see. Needlepoint is a perfect example of the tough sell. It may not appeal to everyone, but if you find the right angle, you can give it universal appeal. You just have to be creative.

How Do I Pitch a Strike of an Idea?

To get your point across to producers, you must prepare to pitch your idea. This is not a difficult process. It's really just a telephone call or a letter telling them that you have an idea for their show. But you'll have to prepare first. The following is a list of things you should do to get off on the right foot with a prospective producer:

- Write a pitch letter. Whether you're pitching a book you authored, or a product you made, or just yourself as an expert, you'll need to have a pitch letter prepared. Make it simple and to the point. Many producers will just skim it, if they read it at all. Use bullet points or large text to highlight important points you want to make.

- Think of angles. As I mentioned earlier, you need to do as much work as you can for the producer. Think of the various ways the producer could do a segment on your idea. Be creative, especially if it's an unusual or seemingly uninteresting topic for television. Thought over long enough, anything can be made interesting to the average viewer.

- Prepare materials for mailing and faxing. Now that you know what you are going to say, put it on paper. Don't let this part slow you down. Don't spend hours or days laboring over each word that you write. Like I said, most producers will only skim the information. If you want to write a separate sheet outlining a biography or "bio" of yourself, make that a part of your materials. If you have or decide to write a sheet or two that goes into extended detail on whatever it is that you are hoping to promote, also make that a part of the materials. When you are all done, you'll have a press kit

- Include the product.[1] If it's a book, CD, or product you are trying to promote, be prepared to send whatever it is along with all of your other press information. Producers will need to see something tangible to be read, tried out, or sampled for themselves. Although you have to plan on giving a lot of this away, never to be returned to you, sending it to them is crucial. All publicists do this. Because you are acting as your own publicist, you need to be seen in the same professional light if you want to taken seriously.

---

[1] Remember, to save money, you can still be selective about who receives your product. You can develop an A and B TV media list. See Linda Radke's tips in Part 1 of this book. *LFR*

Wherefore Art Thou, Program?

Now that you have prepared your press materials, you are ready to make your contacts. What you'll need to do is make a list of where you will go with your pitch. Think about the outlets that you will want to pitch yourself to. Make a list of the television stations in your area. Then, make a list of national television shows that you think you would be right for. Making a good match is a big part of it. You wouldn't pitch "This Old House" a segment story idea on a new book you have written titled, *The Truth About President Harry S. Truman*.

Call information to get the numbers of the television stations in your area. Some may have websites where you can find out about the various shows that a channel offers. Call the stations and ask for a segment producer or booker on that show.

If you are considering calling a national show, there are a couple of things to keep in mind. Producers of national shows will usually prefer an in-studio guest over one available via satellite from another city. Think about where you are in relation to where they are. Many of the national morning talk shows are located in New York. Would it sway them if you planned a trip to New York? These are bargaining chips that you need to think about and consider.

Ring-A-Ling!

Making phone calls is probably the most crucial part of the process. Without phone calls, most of your work will be done in jest. This is how you start the process, and how you end it. This is the way a producer gets a sense of who you are.

Don't be afraid. You never know with whom you're dealing on the other end. You may get someone who is nice and is genuinely interested in what you have to say. Or you may get a cold and uninterested person who will dismiss you and your segment idea in a heartbeat. Either way, without a phone call, your pitch letter has a good chance of becoming recycled paper, and the product you've sent along with it will end up in the trash or collecting dust underneath their desk. That's why I suggest making an initial "interest" call to find out if you should even send or fax the material you've put together.

To help guide you through the call, you have the pitch letter, which you have spent time thinking about. Try to be short and to the point. Let the producer know that you think you have an interesting segment idea for the show, and be prepared to follow up the conversation with a fax or mailing of more information. Follow up with another call to see if there is continued interest. Don't worry about bothering the producer. Unless you are calling more than three times a week, you are not a bother. You are just someone who is interested in getting on the show. Most producers understand that. Listen to the tone in their voice. You'll know if they feel that you are calling them too much. Many times, producers are thankful for the reminder.

Attention Seekers

Do your research. I'm not saying that you need to spend hours, days, weeks, or months researching possible outlets for publicity. The most important thing that you need to know is to WHOM you are pitching. By "whom" I mean the particular style and content of any given program. I can't tell you how many people call me with no idea what kind of program I work on. If you watch a show for five minutes, you'll know that a new spongy toy you've designed to turn colors in the bath may not be the best topic for a political debate show or a cooking program. This is obviously a ridiculous example, but the point is clear. It is important to have done some homework if you want your pitch to be taken seriously. Also, you'll be saving yourself a great deal of time in the long run. Like most people pitching ideas and, with any luck, appearing on television, you have a full-time job and do not need to waste your time on fruitless phone calls.

You will impress the producer if you say something about either the program, or the program's host(s). That shows that you've taken enough interest to watch. A little "schmoozing" never hurts. In fact, if the producer can be "warmed up," you greatly increase the chances that he or she will truly listen to your pitch.

If you've already received some publicity, say a newspaper article, use it in your pursuit for more publicity. Send a copy along with your pitch letter to a producer. It will give you more credibility. It shows the producer that someone else thought that you were interesting, and they should, too.

It should be noted that some print and television outlets carry more weight than others. If you boast about being written up by the local *Pennysaver*, it will not do as much for you as say, an article in *USA Today*. The same goes for television. If you have been interviewed on "Oprah" and "The Today Show," play it up. Use it to help get you on other shows. Saying that you did an hour on the local cable-access channel will most likely not impress a producer.

There are ways, however, to get around this. If you have an article that was written by a small paper, cut out the article by itself. If it is from the local *Pennysaver*, cut the name of the newspaper off the sheet. If it is a small, yet respected paper, keep the name on the page in one spot, or write it in. If you made an appearance on a small television show, and are proud of your performance, offer the tape only if you think it will help get you booked on a show. Make sure to let the people you're sending it to know what to expect before they see it. Poor production values could end up making you look bad.

Don't Sweat the Setbacks

Just as in any other part of life, there will be setbacks in this process. You will probably at some point encounter a producer with a bad attitude, or you may deal with someone who says they are interested, but aren't, or you will at some point receive rejection. Just know that it is part of the process. My only advice is to do your best to be diplomatic and polite while talking to producers on the phone. Keep making efforts. Another producer may put you on a show, which might lead to a newspaper article, which might lead to a booking on a show by a producer who wouldn't give you the time of day before.

What do you do if you leave a message for a producer, and you don't get a call back? This can be frustrating. They might not have returned your call because they became very busy for a few days and just forgot. Call back and try to connect with the person. Don't give up until they have told you themselves that this is not something they want to do.

You Are Your Message

It should be no surprise to you that what you say and how you say it conveys a lot of information to a producer. Talking with someone on the phone and talking with that same person in person is quite different. Think of a telemarketer's job. It is an extreme challenge to get a stranger to buy something over the phone. The telemarketer is not a face, or a person, to the people on the other end of the line. The telemarketer is just a voice, and so the process is impersonal. You are like a telemarketer. You are on the phone, talking to somebody who doesn't know you, to make a pitch, to sell your idea. Especially when you don't know the person, connecting with them can be difficult and grabbing their attention, a challenge.

Without a doubt, you will be dismissed if, out of nervousness, you:

- have trouble putting sentences together well;
- have difficulty elaborating on whatever you are trying to promote or talk about on television;
- talk too softly or talk too loudly;
- go off on strange tangents that make it hard for the producer to follow what you are saying;
- read verbatim from your press information; or
- sound like a low-energy person.

If you exhibit any of these awkward characteristics or any other signs of social ineptness, you will scare a producer and most likely will not appear on the show. For example if you come off as someone with low energy, the producer likely will think that you will appear that way on the air. The producer can't take any risks. The people he or she books on the show reflect how good, or in this case how bad, he or she is at his or her job, which is finding interesting guests for interesting segments.

Help, I Need Somebody!

At this point, you might be thinking, "Should I get a publicist?" Trying to appear on television is important to you, and you don't want to do something that will keep you from getting what you want. You may ask yourself, "What if I don't have the right energy on the phone?" Well, you don't need a publicist to get yourself on television. Of course, it doesn't hurt, but that's not why you bought this book. If you come to the telephone conversation fully prepared, if you're confident, and if you've prepared by putting yourself in the producer's position to try to find out what they want, you'll be okay. Once you've done these things, you will increase your chances of landing a spot on the producer's show, giving you exposure to a large number of people. After getting on that first show, you will have gained the credibility you'll need to get booked for other television interviews. It only gets easier from that point. You'll become experienced, and learn something from each interview that you do.

What should you do if you are canceled, or bumped, from a show? Try to find out why you were taken off the show. Do everything you can to get yourself booked again, short of being a pest. Be as flexible as possible. If a producer took the time and energy to book you the first time, it was because he or she thought you were worthy of being on the show. You most likely were bumped due to reasons beyond the producer's control.

Hi Mom, I'm on TV!

OK. Let's say that you made the connection. A producer wants you to come on and talk about your area of expertise. You aren't bumped from the show. You figure that you'll mark the day on your calendar, show up, answer a few questions, walk away, and viewers at home will respond to what you say. It's sounds simple enough, but it's not quite that easy.

Be Our Guest

What does being a good guest mean? If all goes well for you, being a good guest means that you will be someone who will be called again. You'll be someone who is recommended to other producers by the person who booked you. And many times, being a good guest means that you were able to get your point through to the viewer. Before you appear for your interview, you should prepare some objectives for yourself that are clear. This way you will have some guidelines to say everything you want. (Many times you won't end up covering it all, but it's good to have a game plan.) On many shows, the producer will call you up a couple of days (or sometimes a couple of weeks) before the interview to confirm everything with you and may also conduct a pre-interview. In this pre-interview, the producer will prepare you by asking questions that will be similar to the host's (or hosts') questions. This is not always done. But if it is done, two good reasons for doing it are: 1) The producer can get a better idea of how you will respond on television, and 2) it will give you an idea of what will happen during the segment. Often, however, the pre-interview is in the form of a casual conversation between you and the producer. Don't worry if you're not given a pre-interview (and don't subsequently bother the producer for one); you will be informed before the show of how the segment will go, and what will be expected from you. The best preparation you can do is by yourself. If you need to, go back over all of your press information. This will help to highlight the important points in the interview.

You definitely don't want to be labeled as a needy guest. One of the biggest pitfalls is becoming an overeager or needy guest. You could end up shooting yourself in the foot. If this is your first time being interviewed, great. Don't think that just because you've been booked on the show, your new friend, the producer, can speak to you constantly about every worry and concern. If you have some questions, jot them down, and try to ask them all at once. High-maintenance guests are the first ones who find themselves cut on a busy day, or end up getting their airtime shortened. Be confident. You got this far; you'll be fine.

Here are a few other things you should keep in mind to ensure that this interview won't be your last. If you follow these tips, you will ensure a successful appearance and will increase your chances of being called to appear again. You will, at the very least, have a good tape of your interview that you can show to future producers:

- Be on time to the studio.
- Match your style of clothing to the style of the show.
- Look well-groomed.
- Be a high-energy guest.
- Act friendly and cooperate with the host(s).
- Elaborate fully—don't give one-word responses.
- Use short anecdotes to illustrate ideas.

Get a Hold of Those Reins!

During the interview, it's all about control. Many people think that an interview is a meeting between people where one asks questions, and the other gives answers. Even though it is the job of the television anchor or host to lead you through the interview, it is important to take some of the control. It's important to think about where everyone is coming from when they meet in an interview situation.

We've established that you are there because you want to get a message across. Ultimately you either want people to buy your book, product, or service or you want to persuade the wider audience to agree with you on some particular topic you have been brought on to discuss.

The interviewer is sitting down to do one of thousands of interviews. Who knows how much preparation this person has done this day? The interviewer might not have done any.

Don't just sit there and answer questions. A good guest is always thinking about the big picture. Just like a good politician, you need to come to the table with an agenda and an idea of what you want to say. Just because you weren't asked a specific question that would allow you to make a point doesn't mean that you can't bring that point up. You should be cooperative enough to answer any question that the interviewer asks, but you can also redirect the flow of conversation to allow you to make the points that you want to make. Practice at home if you need to. Find out how much time you'll be getting for the interview. The average would be from three to six minutes. That may seem short to you, but to the people who are at home with their remote controls, it is a very long time. Do what you can to get enough of your points across to entice viewers to find out more about you.

What do you do if you were told that you would get six minutes of air time and you only get three? The answer: deal with it. You should be happy to get the opportunity to be on television and the air time for a little self-promotion. Make the most out of the three minutes that you do get. Give some great information and leave the viewer wanting more. You might end up with a better segment.

Could You Mention That 101 More Times?

"Watch me hold up my book while I answer your question. ... Gee, that's something that I cover in Chapter Two of my NEW BOOK!" If you want this television interview to be your last, you'll become an overzealous promoter. Every television producer expects you to throw in your plug, but exercise a little restraint. There's nothing worse than a guest who has to drop their plug into every answer they give. You may think that this will help viewers remember who you are, but the result will be to anger those who have given you the opportunity to be on television, and give viewers the feeling that you are trying to sell them something instead of giving them information. Selling is for commercials, not television shows (even though you are obviously there to promote your product). Just try to remember that the producer wants you there to make for an interesting segment for his or her viewers. You don't need to do shameless plugging. It is standard for the interviewer to mention your plug at the beginning or, at least, at the end of the interview. In addition, it will be listed on screen below your name to let viewers know who you are.

There are ways to seamlessly work your plug into the conversation. One guest might say, "I did a study for the book which found..." Viewers are now saying to themselves, "Hmm. That's interesting. What book did this person write?" This technique is something you'll have to work on. I recommend doing it only a couple of times during the interview, and in the most subtle way you can.

One Good Hand Returns Another

I talked a little bit about how being a good guest will help you in the long run. You would be surprised how the media plays off one another. Many television producers get their ideas from newspaper articles. And many newspaper writers watch television for their ideas. Do your best to get as much information out there as you can. Try to make it interesting. If you can make it sound interesting to your friends and family, you'll be able to make it interesting for the viewers and those who might want to book you on another show.

That's All, Folks

The best advice I can give? Don't worry and don't stress. If you think that you have something that people will want to hear about, and if you truly believe that it is interesting, the people you talk to will also. As long as you do the preparatory work outlined here, you will shine under those studio lights. Don't forget to enjoy the process. Good luck!

I was out fishing recently in a well-stocked lake. I hooked a big one, but it got away when my rod broke. As Larry Carlson explains, broadcasting is as well-stocked with opportunities for publicity as that lake was stocked with fish. However, you need to have good bait and the right rod to land the fish (a good project to promote and an interesting angle on it). Don't let the big one get away.

There's an Opportunity Born Every Minute

By Larry Carlson

P.T. Barnum would have loved today's electronic media stage and the hype that surrounded the onset of the new millennium. Not because there's a chance that more suckers than ever are being born each minute, but because contemporary life is spawning more pseudo-events and more media coverage of everything than even the master showman, publicist, and father of hype could have imagined.

Thankfully, those of us seeking publicity for our clients or ourselves don't have to tout Tom Thumb or a three-ring circus to garner radio and television coverage.

If you have a story to tell (and we all do!), there's never been a better time to showcase it on television and radio.

Whether we're considering national hosts such as Oprah Winfrey and Howard Stern or the noontime gardening show in

Keokuk, Iowa, programmers are constantly faced with the challenge of attracting and holding viewers and listeners. If they don't come through, it's a case of "fifty-seven channels, and nothin' on," as Bruce Springsteen growled in protest of wasted airwaves.

In any given TV market, from New York, New York to Laredo, Texas, you have an abundance of local news programs. Less than thirty years ago, local television news was considered somewhat of a "loss leader" by many stations. They provided a couple of half-hour news programs, usually to usher in the network's afternoon news and later, to top off the prime-time slate. Federal Communications Commission regulations dictated that outlets serve up certain quantities of local news programming as part of their community responsibility.

Maybe it was the replacement of film by videotape, thus providing immediate playback and instant editing capabilities, that showed the purveyors of local news that their programs could be profitable.

A boom era erupted in the 1980s and continued through the 1990s, and many television stations in medium and large markets now supply viewers with five to eight locally produced news and "info-tainment" programs each day, some of them even lasting sixty minutes. Why? Because these programs have shown the capability to earn huge sums of money in advertising dollars.

Radio has undergone radical changes in recent years, most notably in the wake of FCC deregulation. Whereas all stations had previously kept some semblance of a news department—often with just one-minute news capsules several times each day—because of FCC regulations, now, for the most part, only news/talk formats offer local news, except in small, one-station cities.

In the larger markets, that means news programming on only one or two radio stations. That's bad news for promoting anything.

Here's the good news. Those stations are running news and talk, mostly talk, on a wall-to-wall basis, twenty-four hours a day, seven days a week. That means there's more space available than before for us to gain publicity on concepts, products, and personalities, free of charge. And if you're just wishing to get the word out about an event, virtually all stations still run a community calendar.

Given all these factors, programmers are faced with a daily—sometimes hourly—quest to stack programs with hot topics and entertaining guests.

They need content. They need fresh ideas and different faces. That's your cue.

Strike a Match

Your first move is to strike a match between the available electronic media outlets and the target audience of your message. Eliminate the stations that don't fit. It doesn't make sense to scatter-shoot when it comes to publicity. A financial message won't match a top-forty radio format's listeners, and a notice about a ten-year high school reunion shouldn't be aimed at easy-listening or classical-music stations, which draw an older audience. Get to know your area's stations and programs. Then, pick your spots.

Don't forget that the time of day matters for broadcast exposure. When do you want your message to air, based on your target audience?

"Dayparts" is radio jargon for the different times of day, and programming is designed to reflect what listeners and viewers are doing at a particular time of day. Morning and afternoon "drive times" are still the most coveted radio slots for reaching adults on their way to and from work. The evening hours for television watching are known as "prime time" for good reason.

But remember. The work force and workplace evolve continually. It's not as easy to pigeonhole the public as it once seemed. There are millions of graveyard-shift workers listening to radio after midnight, and college students appear to have replaced June Cleaver and the idealized 1950s housewives as the key target audience for daytime television.

Who to Tell?

Once you've narrowed your list of desirable stations or programs within those stations, you need to reach the right people.

- If you're trying to place yourself or a client on a talk show, you need the producer or an assistant producer of the program.

- If you're trying to get on the news, you'll want the news director or assignment editor. It's also still possible that you'll seek a producer. These are the people who largely write the news and fit the whole program puzzle together.

An important note here: be certain to get correct spellings of your contacts' names from the receptionist you speak with. Get their titles and learn to pronounce their names. It's such a simple thing, but it can make or break the chance to tell your story.

Get Your Story Out

Now, it's crunch time. Your first message to someone in charge should be a brief news release, media advisory, or query letter sent via mail, e-mail, or fax, or hand delivered to the station lobby. They are very busy people, so it's crucial to get to the point. It's also important to give plenty of warning if you need coverage of an upcoming event. A month's notice is ideal.

Be brief, but DO attach enough information (in the form of a fact sheet, bio or the like) for them to understand the who, what, where, and when of what you're pitching. If you're stumping for a TV gig, enclose a photo or, if possible, a video clip of a previous television appearance. Similarly, send an audio tape to radio stations in order to create interest.

When soliciting television news coverage, not just a studio guest shot, it is imperative that you think visually. Television demands dramatic backdrops, color, and movement. Sell your TV contact on the visual aspects of your story. Ever notice how campaigning politicians are always seen with backgrounds of busy harbors, whistle-stop trains, and amber waves of grain? Think visually.

Here's another tip. If you have a prop that is pertinent to the story, sell that idea, as well. Television consultants have hammered it into reporters that, in a strong visual package or live shot, they must "show and tell," utilizing props, not just wild hand gestures or a slow stroll to dramatize the script. So uncover the artifacts, the evidence, or the spoils of victory. Providing the station with an interesting prop for your story could convince them just how compelling it is.

Follow Up

There are no absolutes when it comes to timing your follow-up phone call to check on the status of your mailed pitch. Generally, you should wait two to five days before trying to confirm the arrival of your initial message.

Two things here: first, do not even think about cold calling a news director, producer, or the like. Leave that to salespeople.

Second, be prepared. If you do get in contact with someone in charge, be ready to outline your proposal if they haven't seen it or their memory needs a jog. If the station is already somewhat interested, have the necessary information and phone presentation to close the deal. Go into your call with plenty of ammunition.

If you have trouble making contact with the desired person, persistence pays. Keep trying. Just don't leave 200 voice-mail messages in a single morning. Check in daily.

Eventually, you will get a "yes" or "no." Radio and television people are used to having to work themselves to track down sources and leads. Your persistence, within reason, is expected.

Preparation Pays

Once you succeed in landing coverage, there's no such thing as too much preparation. If you or a client will appear on television, wear appropriate apparel. Avoid white clothing and extremely busy patterns. Even more importantly, use mock interviews to practice and be ready for any questions. If your story deals in controversy, beware of questions designed to put you on the spot. Regardless of the subject matter or the radio or TV outlet, much of what you say won't be used unless you are interviewed live. So make each remark count. Learn to speak in sound bites, as it were. That is to say, be clear and concise, and if appropriate, snappy with your answers. News stories require ten-second type responses. Talk-show guests can afford to elaborate and expand their responses. Stress poise and articulation in getting ready for coverage. The camera doesn't blink, and it's wise to always consider the microphone on. Always.

Attention-Getting Ideas

If you, your company, or clients don't have an obvious hook for catching media attention, that doesn't mean that coverage isn't available. Remember that most news and talk programs focus on planned events or pseudo-events such as meetings, celebrations, speeches, and press conferences. Except for fires, accidents and disasters, most stories don't "just happen." Most stories and individuals get attention because media outlets are contacted, cajoled, and convinced by publicity people doing their homework to match media with audience and sell a story or story angle.

There are dozens of ways to create opportunities that can earn media attention. Here are just a few reliable methods for steering the media your way:

■ Link your story to current events and localize what might not otherwise be covered by area media.

■ Tie in with a holiday.

■ Put on a special event.

■ Get on the agenda of a local governing body, with an award, commendation or grievance.

■ Celebrate a company anniversary.

Opportunities Are Vast

Don't ever forget that there are more broadcast outlets than ever before, with more programming time to fill. Take advantage of it.

In the new millennium, every station is looking for good ideas and intriguing guests. P.T. Barnum would have it made. After all, only a sucker wouldn't take advantage of all this opportunity for publicity.

Talk radio continues to be one of the most dominant formats in radio, from the "shock jock" style of Howard Stern and the sports-talk stations to the intellectual NPR style to the call-in advice shows. Bobbie Thomas, a talk show host herself, explains how to take advantage of these opportunities to talk about your project.

Radio Marketing Made Simpler

By Bobbie Thomas

As a radio talk-show host in central Florida, I interview a lot of people, from celebrities and politicians and other newsmakers to policy-makers in the White House. Author interviews are among my favorite types of interviews, and I know what I'm looking for in selecting writers and books.

The first thing I seek in a book is something that interests me. Then, the book must have a subject that will relate to the listener or bring them to the program after advance promotion. Self-help books, do-it-yourself books, medical books, personal accounts of survival, cookbooks, books on gardening, and humor books are almost guaranteed to hold audience interest and generate calls. Sports and fiction are problematic and, often, seasonal. Autobiographies depend on the subject. A personal recollection from a famous singer, for example, will usually work, but one from their sibling probably won't.

Be Available

Serendipity sometimes plays a part in the selection of authors. If you make yourself available for last-minute interviews and respond immediately to inquiries, you'll get more exposure in more places. Current events or the release of government or medical studies may relate directly to your story and expertise and make you more desirable to the producer looking for guests.

For example, we did a series on hate crimes and the shootings that took place in Chicago allegedly related to the World Church of the Creator. I had already booked the Cantor Leo Fettman, the author of *Shoah: A Journey from the Ashes—A Personal Story of Triumph Over the Holocaust.* The juxtaposition of events and topic were perfect for calls from both sides. But even if I hadn't scheduled a Holocaust survivor, it would have been the perfect time to find one to complete the series and add impact to the issue. That's where being available becomes paramount. If we can't find you, you don't get your story out.

Make Yourself Visible

For many authors, their publisher is their best promoter. We get many of our contacts and leads from publishers such as Five Star Publications, who bring us new authors on a regular basis and who will provide extra promotion by offering book copies to us for giveaway or local sale. Some publishers also list their authors in media publications such as the *Radio-TV Interview Report,* or with fax fliers such as the Great Guests Newsletter, *The Inside Straight* and *Hot Guest, Inc.* As a self-promoter, you might think about these lists as well. They are important places for you to be if you want to get noticed.

To begin promoting yourself to radio, tune into local talk shows in your area and make direct approaches to the producers or hosts. We find some authors that way and many of our small-business stories come directly from telephone calls to the station. You should be prepared to provide the interviewer with a biography and basic background on your work. It is also beneficial to you to have a list of prepared questions that will bring out points you consider important. Such lists give the interviewer an outline and will make you a better interview.

Practice, Practice

For the interview itself, there are three major requirements for the best performance. They are practice, practice, and practice. Talking is different from writing. Some authors do both without problems, but some become tongue-tied or nervous at the prospect of a microphone in their face. One way around that fear is to do telephone interviews. Everyone can relate to talking on the phone and most don't freeze up one on one. Your prepared question list can be your best friend, especially if you also prepare a matching answer list. You can always deviate from it or follow threads suggested by either list or injected by the host—but in the event of brain seizure or stage fright, you've got what amounts to a working script.

If I could give you only one tip for successful interviews, it would be NO ONE-WORD ANSWERS! Nothing kills an on-air interview or loses listeners faster than an author who doesn't answer in paragraphs instead of monosyllables. If you can't talk spontaneously and at length about yourself and your work, you might want to consider a different venue.

Radio is not a visual medium. We create our environment via live words much the way you do in print. The main difference is real time. A reader can reflect and imagine. A listener needs constant input to maintain their interest. What would a blank page do to the continuity of your book? In radio, dead air is a blank page and a cardinal sin. A good host will be able to bail you out of a pregnant pause, but it may take practice for you to keep talking and making sense at the same time. Short answers also make for short interviews, which won't do you as much good as a long one with substance and feedback.

Interview Tips Recap

1. PRACTICE speaking. Use your friends and family as guinea pigs. Make sure you get up at least an hour earlier than your scheduled appearance if you're doing an early morning interview. Your voice may need exercise.

2. Talk to the host before your appearance, if possible. Break the ice. Make a personal connection, if possible.

3. Provide the host with your biography. Be as inclusive as necessary.

4. Provide the host with your own question list well in advance.

5. Prepare a matching answer list for yourself. You can provide that to the host as well for continuity.

6. Be prepared for any question from your list or biography.

7. Be prepared to answer questions from call-in listeners. They may differ significantly from what you prepared.

8. Time your questions and answers for interview length. If you know how far you can get in fifteen minutes or thirty minutes, you can assist in directing your interview to your best advantage.

9. Don't panic. It's only radio. It's just a conversation with a fellow being who wants you to succeed.

10. PRACTICE! PRACTICE! PRACTICE!

Book Sales through Radio

I'm in a unique situation. My station is an all-talk format that features a live shopping show that airs six days a week. We can take the author's book beyond the single interview exposure and multiply it several times by offering their book for sale on our shopping shows. This local sale also includes a matching amount of commercials that we produce and air in exchange for the value of the books provided by the author or publisher. This keeps the interest up beyond the interview and airs the title, author, and availability for up to two weeks after the initial appearance.

Our shopping show also extends to an Internet site. We can place your book there for the entire planet to see and purchase. It's one more exposure and it's all barter—books for commercials. Everybody wins. We get a few bucks that pay for your commercial. The listener gets a bargain. And your book gets attention. We also keep all your information available for listeners who call later and want to know where to find you. You may be able to find similar setups at other stations and it's something to keep in mind when you are looking for opportunities.

Premium Promotions

Books may also be offered as premiums or giveaways to promote the interview in advance or generate callers during the show. You can send them to the host before the program airs or tell the callers how to get them directly from you after the show. (Your product doesn't have to be a book. Video, audiotapes, or CDs, among others, are legitimate interview subjects.)

Small Business on Radio

All of these tips and techniques also work for small businesses. Every small business has a story and many of them make great show topics. The process of contact and exposure are the same. If you are a small-business owner without a publicity department or budget, you need to promote yourself by going the direct contact route previously described.

Make Your Materials Complete

As an author or as a small-business owner, make sure you get *all* your contact information into your biography, question sheet, answer sheet, and on your fax cover sheet. You'd be amazed how many people forget this most basic concept.

It's also the Internet age, so get an e-mail address at the very least and a website if you can. Nothing is faster than the Internet or permits more information to move anywhere.

Remember, Hosts Differ

Not all talk shows are the same. Some hosts never shut up and some want you to do all the talking. If you get a rude or self-centered host, don't get discouraged. Remember there's no such thing as bad publicity.

Joe Sabah, who has sold more than 22,000 copies of his book *How to Get the Job You Really Want and Get Employers to Call You*, considers talk radio to be just about the perfect vehicle for promoting books. When you're done reading what he has to say, you may want to check out his website at **www.JoeSabah.com** for his suggestions on the perfect wardrobe for talk-show interviews.

How to Promote Yourself on Radio Talk Shows All Across America Without Leaving Your Home or Office

By Joe Sabah

Tom Peters, author of *Thriving on Chaos and In Search of Excellence*, wrote,

> When you are interviewed on TV you may get three to five minutes. When you are interviewed by a newspaper, the reporter gets to write what they 'think' you said. But when you are interviewed on talk radio, you get thirty to sixty uninterrupted minutes to chat with the host, and answer questions from people calling in. You get to give out your 800 number for orders.

Instant response—you heard it from the pro.

Whether you have a product to sell or a story to tell, talk radio is the easiest and most profitable avenue to make your dreams come true (and your cash register ring).

Picture This Scenario

You're at home. The phone rings.

Radio Talk Show Producer: "Good Morning, Joe. This is Charlie Talk Show Producer with WXYZ. I have Sally Talk-Show-Hostess waiting on the line for your interview. Are you ready?"

Joe: "Yes I am, Charlie. How long will I be on the air with Sally?"

Charlie: "About 30 minutes, minus commercials."

Joe: "Will she have listeners calling in?"

Charlie: "Most likely. Hold on please. We're just 30 seconds away from air time."

Sally Radio-Talk-Show Hostess: "And now radio station WXYZ welcomes our special guest, Joe Sabah. He joins us this morning by telephone from Denver, Colorado. Joe co-authored the book, *How to Get the Job You Really Want and Get Employers to Call You.* Good morning, Joe, and welcome to station WXYZ's 'Morning Talk with Sally.'"

Joe: "Good Morning, Sally. It's my pleasure to be with you and your listeners."

Sally: "Joe, your book has a most intriguing title. Would you tell us how you came up with this idea and how our listeners can use these job-getting techniques?"...

Twenty-eight minutes and several callers later:

Sally: "Joe, our time has just flown by. One last question: how can our listeners of WXYZ get a copy of your book?"

Joe: "I have a toll-free number to order the book today. It will be sent out the same day the call is received via U.S. Priority Mail. All for only $17.95, when you call 1-800-945-2488. The number again is: 1-800-945-2488."

Sally: "Thanks again, Joe. I am looking forward to having you back again soon."

A dream? No. This scenario has been repeated more than 630 times—all without leaving my home.

As a result, I have sold over 22,750 copies of my book at the retail price of $17.95. That's more than $376,000 in book sales, all at full retail.

Why Would You Want to be on Radio Talk Shows?

- You love to talk
- You have something to say to the world
- You want more publicity
- You want to increase your sales and profits
- You have a book or audiotape or videotape to offer

What's the Secret to Getting on Radio Talk Shows—and Profiting from Them?

1. Passion
2. Database
3. 800 number and Visa, MasterCard, and American Express acceptance

1. About Passion

First you need a passionate desire to tell your story. I recall Dale Carnegie's admonition to

Only, only, only speak on something that you've earned the right to speak about... through either your experience or education.

Every year for the past ten years I have been updating my talk-show database. Each time I talk with either a host or producer, I ask the same question: "Exactly what are you looking for?" The answers are always the same: **either "free information" or "something controversial."** Recently, however, I noticed that most radio producers have added a third category.

"We'd really like **someone who is passionate about their subject."** That's the key: passion. Passion for your subject. The passion to want to help listeners of talk radio.

2. About Databases and Marketing

The medium called talk radio is a starving monster. Radio talk-show hosts and producers are constantly looking for great guests. It's your job to let them know you are out there. Where do you get a list of radio stations willing to interview guests by phone? Visiting the library, you'll find *Broadcast Yearbook*, a directory of all the 11,600-plus radio stations in the United States and Canada, and *Bacon's* publishes a directory of radio stations. But any printed directory is at least six months old and will be dated by the time you get to it.

I developed my database over ten years by religiously updating by phone every six months. I now have 850 talk shows in that database.

Booking Shows

Once you have a database of radio stations that have talk shows, you need to fine-tune your marketing plan. How are you going to reach these talk shows? In the 1970s and 1980s, press kits were popular. In the 1990s, the telephone was the best way to book talk shows. Now in the 2000s, I've discovered there is also the technology of broadcast fax.

A one-page sales letter (not a press or media release) gets the job done by fax. We're living in a fast-paced world, so your sales letter must have all the components to grab the host or producer's immediate attention. It must be captivating enough for them to call you before they put the fax down.

But the very best method of achieving results in booking radio talk shows is to use the telephone and call the radio stations. I have found that it helps to have a script. The following is a sample.

First call:

Receptionist: "Radio Station KXYZ."

You: "May I speak with _____ (usually the producer), please?

"Hello, _____, my name is _____.

I understand that you are in charge of scheduling guests for the _____ show. Is that correct?

(In selling, you want your prospect to say "Yes" early—and often.)

"The reason for my call, _____ (their first name) is: "I am the author of a book on the subject of _____, or titled: _____. I believe this information could help your listeners."

(Give them three quick benefits here.)

1. _____

2. _____

3. _____

"Is this the type of subject that you and your host are looking for?" or "Could this subject help the listeners of your show?"

TIPS: The odds of your getting through to the host or the producer on your first call are pretty slim.

When you call the station you may get a response such as, "He/she is not available. Would you like to leave a message on his/her voice mail?" Just remember this phrase:

The person who makes the call stays in control.

Rather than leave messages on voice mail or with the station's receptionist, you will want to say, "No, thank you. What is the best time for me to call back?" So your first round of calls will be to schedule telephone appointments for the next day.

Your first call will have taken about thirty to forty-five seconds. If you are at ten cents per minute on your long-distance service, this call cost you about five to seven cents.

Just keep in mind that radio talk shows and their hosts need you! There is a tremendous need for guests every day of the year. I calculate 780 guests a year per host.

Who's the Teacher and Who's the Student?

Recently, I received a one-page fax from a client/friend in Minnesota who had recently purchased my Radio Talk Show System, which includes the database of stations I have collected. In less space than it took to write a letter, he explained how he uses his computer to broadcast-fax about fifty to sixty one-pagers every Sunday evening. He went on to explain that when telephone rates are lowest, he is able to fax a one-pager for less than the postage for a postcard. When I asked him where he got that idea, he asked me, "Isn't that why you've included the fax numbers for most of the stations?"

Hmmm, who's the teacher and who's the student?

It seems he gets two to three radio talk shows booked each week using this system. Pretty effortless, wouldn't you say? The bottom line? First, you will need a computer, modem, and software that will allow you to send the same message to a number of people. Finally, you'll need to test, test, test!

Another way to handle broadcast fax is to let a professional service handle this project. For only twenty cents per page (which includes long-distance charges), fax-broadcast services can send out 950 one-pagers in about fifteen minutes. Call me at 1-800-945-2488, for more details.

Postcards Work!

Back in 1979, I came up with the idea for the Gold Form, a real attention-grabber in direct mail. Today, I use it as a giant postcard to send to radio stations and producers. Just think, all you have to do is put a first-class stamp plus a mailing label on a card and drop it in the mail. No envelope, no cover letter is required. And when your host or producer receives this giant postcard, it's open and ready to read.

This 5½" × 8½" Giant Gold postcard works. I've kept track of results. I got a six percent return, which means that out of every hundred Giant Gold postcards I mailed to radio stations, six of those stations called to book me.

3. The All-Important 800 Number

In this day and age, you can't turn on your TV or radio and listen to a commercial without hearing the closing lines: **"Just call our toll-free number 1-800-123-4567 to order XYZ."** How do you find an 800-number telephone-answering service to take your orders 24 hours a day, 365 days a year? Surprisingly, 800 numbers are relatively inexpensive and are available through AT&T, Sprint or MCI. Check with your local phone company, too.

I also suggest:

1. Ask your telephone-answering service to set you up. The service may already be set up for Visa, MasterCard and American Express. Not only will the service process your orders, but it will also obtain the authorization number from the credit-card company.

2. Or become a credit-card merchant yourself. With this system, you are responsible for writing up the credit-card orders and processing the deposits through your bank. But first you must qualify to become a credit-card merchant.

3. Look into Electronic Data Capture. I have been a credit-card merchant for the past fifteen years and have found this capability a most valuable service to offer buyers of my books, tapes, and seminars. Electronic Data Capture is a system that uses the same type of terminal that retailers such as

restaurants or gas stations use to process credit cards and get authorization. At the end of the day, my bank automatically deposits the total credit-card sales into my business checking account. I don't know how I would have ever done the amount of business I've done without it. It's truly money in the bank.

Structuring a Successful Interview

Believe me when I tell you, there is a BIG difference between just a radio talk-show interview and a successful radio talk-show interview. Here are some tips that I've learned that make the BIG difference.

- Prepare the area (of your home or office) you will be using for your talk-show interviews. This means you should be relaxed, but not too comfortable.

- Get a 25-foot cord for your telephone or invest in a cordless headset, allowing you *total* freedom to walk and talk.

- I find it most stimulating to stand and walk while I am talking on the telephone, especially when I'm being interviewed on a talk show. This is my style in speaking and seminars. You, of course, will develop your own style.

- The next time you get a phone call, sit down. Notice how you sometimes cradle the phone on your shoulder. This may cause your voice to be muffled. Your shoulders may be slouched over, causing your chest cavity to be sunken. Results? A less-than-effective phone call.

- Next call: Stand erect. Hold the handset up to your mouth. Be comfortable. Pace, if that is your style. Notice the difference? More confidence. More power. More sales.

- Always have a copy of your book/material at your fingertips. Paperclip or highlight the passages that you want to quote from. Use Post-It notes to "flag" important passages from your book.

- Keep a glass of water handy. Some speakers suggest warm or even room-temperature water. Coffee? Tea? Not my style, but try it. See what works best for you.

- Post on your wall or desk the three (*only three*) key points that you want to cover in this interview.

Plus, post your 800 number to give to listeners at the end of the program.

Getting Listeners to Call and Order Your Book

I decided that regardless of the length of the show, I would always promise my listeners that they would receive three things from me by staying tuned to the program.

You might be asking, "How can you squeeze all that into a 15-minute talk show?" It's easy. I just keep in mind that my audience of listeners is the most important reason that I am on the show.

Each of these three keys can be covered in two to three minutes, if need be. I can also expand each one into ten to fifteen minutes, if time allows. The expanded version includes additional examples, stories and incidents from seminars that I've conducted.

Of course, when these listeners have written down the three-step formula, they still have the pencil and paper in their hands. So when I give out my 800 number, they are ready to write it down also.

Make sure that the host *and* the producer *and* the switchboard of the radio station all have your 800 number ahead of time. You'd be surprised how many people call the station long after the program is over asking: "How can I reach Joe who was on your station last month?"

Getting Repeat Bookings

Anyone can get a radio talk-show booking one time. The real secret or key to success is being invited back repeatedly. Here's how to get that happening in your life.

First, you want to be so good that you will automatically be invited back. Second, structure your presentation so that you are planting seeds that will sprout in the near future. Seeds like: "I'm sorry we're running out of time. I have so much more to talk about that could help your listeners on KXYZ. I hope we can get together again soon to discuss _____ and _____."

Plus, follow up every program with a handwritten thank-you note. You will not only be remembered but be asked to return repeatedly. I've been on several stations four or five times and plan to become a permanent fixture.

So here I am, living my dream!

Congratulations and best wishes to you as you live your dream and get on radio talk shows all across America.

A Quick and Easy Summary	
Radio Stations	**You**
They call you	You answer your phone
They pay for the call	You get to be interviewed for free
They ask you questions	You provided them with questions
They invite listeners to call in	You answer listeners' questions
They ask for your 800 number	You give them your 800 number
They thank you	You thank them
They hang up	You take orders and put $$$ in the bank
What a Concept!	What a Country!

chapter 4

The Internet

The Internet is an exciting tool for marketing, research and publicity, and it is growing by great numbers each year. Can you afford not to tap into it? As president of BookZone, Mary Westheimer certainly knows the nitty-gritty of Internet book promotion. "Publications are my passion as well as my profession," she says. That passion comes through in the advice she offers.

Net Returns: How the Internet Can Help You Promote and Sell Books

By Mary Westheimer

Although being on the Internet is now simply a part of business, publishers were among the first to recognize the value of this remarkable medium. In fact, a recent BookZone survey of 9,000 publishing websites reports that nearly 79 percent of publishers had sites by 1999, more than any other industry. Today, books are one of the top items sold online.

Being online supports your other promotional, distribution and sales efforts by providing ways to:

- Gather information from and about your audiences
- Stay in touch with your audiences and the press
- Serve as a 24-hour-a-day, 7-day-a-week, domestic and international, retail, and wholesale sales staff and order taker
- Drive traffic to physical sales channels

Making the most of this medium includes getting listed in online bookstores, establishing your own website, and conducting an online campaign that is integrated into your overall marketing plan.

Online Bookstores Want Your Books

Just like "bricks and mortar" bookstores, online bookstores buy wholesale and sell retail. They usually work through distributors and wholesalers, but they will buy directly from publishers, too. Make sure your titles are listed at Amazon (**www.amazon.com**), Barnes & Noble (**www.bn.com**), and Borders (**www.borders.com**), each of which offers online instructions for submission. It can take up to eight weeks to get listed at some of the online bookstores, so start early.

A Good Site Better

Selling through online bookstores is not the same as having your own website. A site allows you to interact with and promote directly to your audiences; sell your books around the clock domestically and overseas (international sales often account for a third of online book sales), which means more income per sale; and increase your revenue stream by "virtually" selling other books, products, and information without having to stock or ship them.

Before you begin building your site, think about what you want it to do and who you want to use it. During the planning process, you might want to write information about your audiences and purposes on a note and post it in front of you to keep focused.

Consider how an online presence can save you time, money, and resources. Such cost-saving uses can be even more valuable than sales! Can you create a showcase for distributors and the media that will save you money in printing and sending out materials? Can you sell parts of your books or other products? Can you gather information from your audience or others for an upcoming project? Can you build mailing lists of people who will be prime targets for future titles?

Here are some other tips to make your site more productive:

- Research other sites in and out of your niche to see what others are doing and how they're doing it. What makes sense for your goals and audience? What looks good and works well? Keep notes about what you liked or disliked about them.

- Unlike printed materials, you don't have to wait until the next printing to make changes to a site, so plan your site development in phases.

- Having your own domain name is not only more professional, it also gives you the ability to change hosts without losing traffic. Most domain names with .com, .net, .org, .edu and .gov "extensions" come from an organization called Network Solutions and should cost you $35 per year (the first two years are paid initially).

- If your titles are nonfiction, don't just try to sell your books. After all, your visitors probably have never heard of you, so you must first establish some credibility and build interest. If possible, focus your site on your subject, not your publishing company or your book. No one but you and your mom really cares about that.

For instance, if your subject is amateur astronomy, you could create a site called Amateur Astronomy Central, and your domain name could be amateurastronomy.com. Your content, then, is about backyard astronomy, using excerpts from your books, media releases, etc. At the bottom of each article, a hotlinked "call for action" (such as "Learn more by ordering Urban Astronomy now!") takes visitors to an interactive order form.

This "PR" approach makes it easier to add new information, get links from other sites that serve your audiences, and sell other products related to your subject.

- Prepare your site for marketing with effective page titles, metatags, page, and text. For more information about these nuances, visit Search Engine Watch at **www.searchenginewatch.com**.

- Keep your site clean and fast-loading. Wally Bock of **www. bockinfo.com** emphasizes that, until you establish value in your audience members' minds, your homepage should load in ten seconds. That means it should be about 40k in size for your average visitor.

- To compete with the online bookstores' price discounting, offer some discount, perhaps fifteen percent, so that visitors feel they are making a good buying decision. You also can offer added value, such as autographed copies and free reports.

- Build site updates into your marketing plan. To keep your site fresh, consider new tips, articles, or sections, or even a graphic makeover.

Here is some of the information you can include on a site:

- Homepage text that positions the site and serves as a menu

- Bibliographic information about your titles (author, publisher, title and subtitle, ISBN, price, page count, binding, size, etc.)

- A brief description of each title

- Excerpts

- Tables of contents

- Author biographies and photos

- Author Q & As

- Reviews and endorsements

- Online media-kit information, such as fact sheets, media releases, tour information, media appearance schedules

- Company contact information, including a logo, toll-free order phone number, direct phone number (important for overseas buyers!), fax number, physical address, "live" (hotlinked) e-mail address

- Wholesale terms or ordering information, if appropriate
- Free information about your subject (facts, tips, etc.)
- Links to other sites of interest to your audience (this is part of site marketing)
- An interactive order form with all ordering information, including domestic and international shipping charges and delivery times, sales tax information, etc.

Mapping Your Online Offense

Once your site is live you must let the world—and especially your audience—know. Offline, integrate your website and e-mail addresses into everything from your printed materials—including your books themselves—to your broadcast appearances.

To avoid "overwhelmitis," divide and conquer your online marketing tasks.

Set goals of, say, five search-engine submissions, five new links, participation in two mail lists and newsgroups per week, then adjust as necessary.

Use a log to track which sites you've already visited and for follow up. You can create an online form that lets you simply cut and paste information. To help, get a free copy of BookZone's Internet Marketing Toolbox at **www.bookzonepro.com/mkttoolbox.html** on the Web.

Your online campaign involves using search engines and indexes, linking, newsgroups, and mail lists, "e-zines," promotional appearances, and strategic alliances.

Setting Up Signposts

Many people start their searches for information at search engines. These giant online indexes also are a good place to begin your marketing.

You can use a submission service, but you're likely to get better results by working your way through the engines in which you want your site listed. The WebStep 100 at **www.mmgco.com/top100.html** will help you start with the top sites, as most traffic comes from them. Each search engine has its own peculiarities, so read their directions and follow them explicitly. **Searchenginewatch.com** can help you compare the engines, although things change so quickly online that you also should read each site's own instructions.

Don't worry too much about getting into the "top 10" listings of those majors—you probably won't, unless your subject is extremely unusual, you pay for a search-engine maximization service, or you have eight hours a day to devote to staying at the top. That lofty location requires assessing the competition, tweaking pages for each engine's preferences, then besting your rivals again and again as they adjust and leapfrog over you. Making sure you are listed—something you need to check on occasionally, as the engines do drop entries—and listed accurately is more important.

Also, be sure you're listed in specialty engines such as BookZone's book-based Literary Leaps at **www.literaryleaps.com** and engines that cover your subject matter. Find the latter by using the search engines themselves, combining your subject matter with the word "directories," "indices" or "indexes" (for instance, "astronomy+indexes" in some engines).

Creating Connections

Setting up links with other sites your audience visits is an excellent way to build recurring traffic. The goal is to get links to your site, and one of the best ways to get them is to put links on *your* site to the site you want a link *from*, a process often called reciprocal linking.

To find appropriate sites, visit search engines (your worksheet helps you check them off). Search them, using each engine's advanced search methods (to narrow your searches and save time) and the keywords people would use to find your site. At each likely prospect, look for a links page and an e-mail address for the site owner—they're usually on the bottom of the homepage or on a contact page—and ask for a link to your site.

Make it easy for them by providing the exact text and code to add the link and by giving them a link in advance. Here's the sort of message you can use to request links:

> Hi. My name is [NAME] and I have a website at [WEB ADDRESS] that offers information about [SUBJECT THAT RELATES TO THEIR SITE]. Because you also provide useful information on that subject, I've already put a link to your site on my site. Accordingly, I'd appreciate a link to my site on your links page. To make it easy for you, may I suggest this copy for the link on your end:
>
> <A HREF="http://www.amateurastronomy.com/">Amateur Astronomy Central</a> has fascinating information about backyard stargazing.
>
> Thank you very much. Please e-mail me at [YOUR E-MAIL ADDRESS] if you have any questions.

Keep your boilerplate request letter handy in a text file or use your e-mail package's stationery function, which lets you save and retrieve frequently used messages. You also can put the code on your links page, and let visitors copy it from there. Visit the Sensible Solutions site's link page at **www.happilypublished.com/links.html** to see an example.

Again, use your log to track your activity. These contacts can come in handy when planning strategic partnerships.

Club Connections

BookZone's publishing-website survey also revealed that, although only 16.8 percent of respondents used newsgroups and mail lists to promote their sites, those who did were happiest with their online traffic. Newsgroups and mail lists are online clubs. Newsgroup members meet on the Internet's USENET, while mail lists (which are often called "listserves" because of a popular mail list program) use e-mail.

Newsgroups have "threads," in which you can see every post on a particular subject. This availability of all the messages is an advantage of newsgroups. Seek out the groups where your audience congregates. Find newsgroups at Excite at **www.excite.com** and Deja at **www.deja.com**. Deja has a special service that e-mails you about specific subjects. Liszt at **www.liszt.com** is a fantastic source for mail lists.

Once you pinpoint some groups that your audience visits, spend a little time, or "lurk," in the newsgroup or mail list. You can do more harm than good by "spamming," or posting blatant advertising in some of them, but by answering questions and offering information—after all, as author or publisher, you are an expert on the subject—you are communicating the value of your books. For example, rather than telling people, "You really should buy this book about backyard astronomy," you'll gain more mileage by delighting someone with the news that they can see meteor showers tonight.

Whatever groups you choose, take a bit of time to learn what is acceptable, contribute, participate, and you will benefit.

Using the Net's Secret Weapon

So if you're only providing information, how do people know about your books? Of every five people who have a website, only one is using one of the Net's most powerful marketing tools: the signature.

A signature is an attachment that automatically attaches onto the end of your messages. Signatures can be used in e-mail and newsgroup postings. One way to use a signature is to convey a marketing teaser. Include your Web and e-mail addresses, phone numbers, and full name.

Keep your signature compact: Net old-timers consider four lines plenty, yet eight lines aren't uncommon. The presentation and spacing are important. I recommend the signature be presented in Courier typeface, and it can be run 10 point. The lines should break as shown below.

```
.-.-.-.-.-.-.-.-.-.-.-.-.-.-.-.-.-.-.-.-.-.-.-.-.-.-.-.-.-.-
BookZone: a secure high-traffic site with the books of hundreds of
publishers http://www.bookzone.com 800/536-6162 mary@bookzone.com

Today's BZ HOTSPOT: AUDIO EDITIONS--More than 7,000 audiobooks at
    http://www.audioeditions.com/
```

I change the last section daily to highlight a different BookZone site to keep my signature interesting. Always use your website's full address, including the "http://" because many e-mail programs allow people to click on a full address and pop right to that site.

Sign Me Up, Scottie

An easy and inexpensive way to keep your products in your audiences' minds, giving you the multiple impressions that are so important in promotion today, is by having your own "e-zine," or electronic newsletter. E-zine response rates are as high as 20 percent, compared with less than one percent for Web banner ads and three to four percent for traditional direct mail. Why? Your e-zine subscribers are receptive because they sign up to receive the information.

To handle your e-zine, you can use the same types of programs used for interactive mail lists we covered previously, even though most e-zines are one-way, which means that only you or someone you authorize can send messages through it. You also can use one of the online services such as eGroups or Topica at **www.egroups.com** or **www.topica.com** to host your e-zine, although they do place ads on the mailings.

Send out a weekly, monthly, or occasional tip. You can send them daily if you want, but keep your timing manageable, at least at first.

Here are some additional e-zine tips:

- Keep your e-zine to about three screens in length
- Double space between paragraphs
- Keep paragraphs to about four lines to give readers' eyes a break
- To deliver longer information, give a capsule, then link to a page on your site, using the full Web address so they can click through to it
- Use alternative characters (////, ****, etc.) and capital letters to indicate headlines
- Include subscribe and unsubscribe information at the end as a courtesy

Once you have enough subscribers, you can even sell advertising. E-zine advertising is surprisingly effective: A study by *Information-Week Daily* found that forty-four percent of readers of text-only newsletters take an action after seeing an ad, and that forty percent visit the advertisers' websites.

Speaking Up

You also can make special appearances on the Net and the online services. America Online, for instance, has live chats for which the hosts are always looking for guests, and you don't have to be an AOL subscriber to appear. Online bookstores such as Barnes & Noble have author chats, too. Use these opportunities to increase awareness of your books, both through your appearances and the chance to send out special announcements to the newsgroups, mail lists, newspapers and others.

Let's Work Together

Strategic alliances with other sites your audience visits take your Net marketing to the next level. For instance, an astronomy club site might like to sell your books. The club can buy and stock them, or merely forward orders to you for drop-shipping after taking a percentage. It's a win-win: both get contact information of potential future customers and save time, money, and other resources by reducing handling.

You also can sell other publishers' books, as well as other products, on your site. You can become what is called an "aggregator," making your site more valuable to visitors because it has all the information and "goodies" on a particular subject. For instance, Amateur Astronomy Central can carry star charts, magazines, flashlights—well, you get the idea.

Striking Research Pay Dirt

An entire book could be written on online research. The vision of the Net becoming the biggest library in the world, on your desktop 24 hours a day, 7 days a week, is finally becoming a reality.

Interested in a specific niche market? You'll likely find its members online, find out what makes them tick, and how to reach them. Sites such as MediaFinder at **www.mediafinder.com** are invaluable for finding publications, and there are hundreds, if not thousands, of such resources online, both domestic and international. Use the Net liberally as a research tool, and you'll likely find riches beyond your wildest dreams.

Tip of the Iceberg

All of these are ways to increase income and awareness of your books. What we are seeing now is the tip of the proverbial iceberg. In the not-too-distant future, we will look back and try to remember what it was like before the Net became an integral part of our lives.

One last important note: things change quickly online so what you see there takes precedence over anything in print.

Larry Fox points out that virtual communities online offer excellent "places" to find people interested in your specific product or topic. He also shows how cross-promotion can be an easy, effective Internet tool.

Cyber-space: There's Plenty to Fill

By Larry Fox

Why promote your book on the World Wide Web?

With the advent of the Internet, there is plenty of space to fill with content. Every day, webmasters are making space where it earlier didn't exist. One of the great benefits of being in the publishing business as either a publisher or an author is that one is creating content, and the Internet needs content. As a content provider (you're no longer just an author), you can advance the promotion of your book by providing websites with an excerpt. There are groups of people with like interests who gather at websites to find and share information on their passions (bird-watching, child care, conspiracies, etc.). These gatherings are called "virtual communities," and they offer great opportunities to promote your book.

The trick is to give these websites something of value in exchange for promoting your title to their members. This is done by offering the site a free excerpt from your book. They exchange one-to-one marketing for free content. It is a win-win situation. This is called a content-linking campaign. It can be extended to any business that can trade intellectual property for promotion.

To Whom Should I Promote Myself?

As stated earlier, there are groups of people out on the Web who congregate at sites that directly relate to the subject matter of your book. I frequent bird-watching sites because I am always on the lookout for new information, new spots to travel to, new equipment, new books, and new links to other sites on the Internet. You can find these groups by searching for them using the major search engines on the Web:

- http://www.yahoo.com
- http://www.altavista.com
- http://www.askJeeves.com
- http://www.hotbot.com
- http://www.alltheweb.com

You can also use one of the many pieces of software that search using multiple search engines such as Copernic (**www.copernic. com**). This type of software is known as a "bot." There is even a website devoted to bots at **www.botspot.com**.

How Do I Find Them?

There is really only one way to find interested readers for your book on the Web. After using a search engine to do a preliminary search for the subject of the book, you'll need to visit the sites you turned up. Most search software will let you save the results of the search as a file. This file is written as an HTML document, better known as a Web page. You can bring the Web page up in your browser and click on each result. You will then be taken to each result of the search.

Figure 1 shows what the first page of the results for "bird-watching" look like. Each heading in the report is the URL (Universal Resource Locator, or Web address) for a website. Click on the heading and you will be able to visit each site. A typical search using Copernic would bring back about 300 sites.

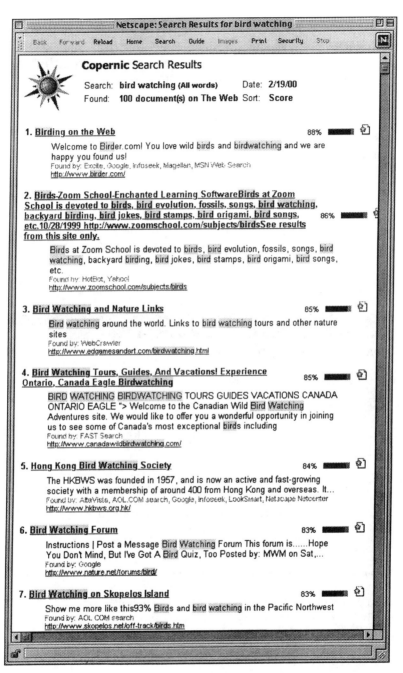

Figure 1

Once you've visited, you can determine whether you want to offer the site a free excerpt. Many sites that show up in the results will turn out to be totally inappropriate and can be discarded. This part of the process is very time-consuming and you may want to outsource it.

By the way, hit counters can lie about the traffic a site gets. If you are using Internet Explorer or Netscape, download the Alexa plug-in from **www.alexa.com** to find out what's really going on with a site. Alexa provides a nice readout of a site's activity: traffic and links in. One good site will lead to others through its own "links" page.

You'll come to recognize the "right" site when you see it.

Sites change fast. You may want to search every couple of weeks for new additions.

Set Up Criteria for Evaluating the Sites

- Is the site on target for my subject?

- Does the site have a book or book review section?

- Does the site have a bibliography page?

- Does the site welcome input and feedback?

- Does the site accept advertising?

- Does the site sell books (i.e., as an Amazon.com associate)?

- Is the site someplace you would want to hang out?

- Does the site represent a community of readers?

You'll learn how to adjust your criteria as you visit sites.

How Do I Contact Them?

Once you've found a site that meets your criteria, you'll need to find the e-mail address of the person on the site responsible for its content. On the site somewhere is an e-mail address of a real person who wants to hear from you because you have "free" content that directly relates to the subject of their site. Sometimes the contact person is *mailto:webmaster@interestingplace.com*. This type of website is a labor of love, and the people who construct them are there because they want to establish a community of other folks who share their world view. Copy and paste each person's e-mail address to a text file for a bulk e-mailing.

Collecting e-mail addresses is a critical step. You must find the right person or you run the risk of "spamming" the wrong person. Be very careful about picking and using e-mail addresses off websites. "Spam" is the Internet equivalent of junk mail, unsolicited mail sent indiscriminately. The difference between spam and junk mail is that people on the Web get extremely angry about spam and may launch a "flame" campaign against you. So being accused of spamming can do more harm than good for the promotion of your book. Remember we are looking for a quality, targeted list, not tens of thousands of unsuspecting recipients. Once you've copied and pasted your list into a text file, you can use that list via your e-mail program to contact the sites that meet your criteria. For a sampling of bulk mail programs, check out **www. davecentral.com/bulkmail.html**.

What Do I Say to Them?

I figure you've got less than ten seconds to get your message across to the recipients of your campaign.

Following is a sample message that you can modify for your own:

Hello

I have recently visited your website and would like to offer you some FREE content of specific interest to your parenting visitors from *Right From Birth; Me, Myself and I* and *Going to School* from Goddard Press.

Even with all the technical advances on the Web, good content remains the best way of making your site continuously engaging. It's my intent to provide you with the best free content available; subject matter that has been chosen with specific regard to your site's focus. I also would like to give your site a reciprocal link on foxcontent.com's "best of category" page.

Meanwhile, please feel free to read the excerpts by following the links at **www.foxcontent.com/Excerpts.htm** and then copy them to use on your own site.

By providing this service free to carefully researched and selected sites, I hope to build a network of reciprocal and like-minded, category-specific websites. If this is successful, and you are happy with the selection, I hope an ongoing relationship with your site can be forged as foxcontent.com continues to supply you with inventive and pertinent content from the books of independent publishers and writers.

If this does not interest you, please let me know. We want to build relationships. If you do not want to be contacted again, please let us know that, too, by e-mailing me personally at **lrfox@foxcontent.com**. I want to create a service of value for everyone involved!

Let me know if you are interested by e-mailing me at **lrfox@ foxcontent.com** or by calling me at 301-699-9744. I look forward to hearing from you.

Best
Larry Fox • **www.foxcontent.com**

The message is brief and truthful and indicates to the webmaster that we are not trying to sell them anything. The subject of the e-mail was "New Parenting Books." A linking campaign is a win-win situation for everyone involved. You get to promote your book to its targeted audience, the website gets much-needed quality content, and the members of the virtual community get the latest book information about their favorite interest. Also, always give the recipients an easy way to be removed from your mailing list.

How Do I Follow Up?

The critical step for successful follow-up is to have the excerpt ready to go. It can either already reside on your own website or it can exist as a plain text file to be sent out as an attachment to your follow-up e-mail. Either way, have it ready to go before you do your mailing. Many ISPs (Internet service providers: America Online, Mindspring, Erols, CompuServe, etc) provide some site space free.

Once a recipient responds that they are interested in using your content, the link is forged. You'll now have the opportunity to establish a long-term relationship with a site that may want to use your content again. Make sure that the excerpt has some kind of link at the end that enables the reader to buy the book (i.e., **amazon.com, barnesandnoble.com**, etc). After all, our primary intent is to increase sales. Submit your page to the search engines so that when someone is out there searching for "bird-watching" they might find your excerpt with its link to **amazon.com**.

References

The Control Revolution: How The Internet is Putting Individuals in Charge and Changing the World We Know, Andrew L. Shapiro (1999, Public Affairs)

Publicity On The Internet: Creating Successful Publicity Campaigns on the Internet and the Commercial Online Services, Steve O'Keefe (1996, John Wiley & Sons)

Hosting Web Communities, Cliff Figallo (1998, John Wiley & Sons)

Business-to-Business Internet Marketing: Proven Strategies for Increasing Profits through Internet Direct Marketing, Barry Silverstein (1998, Maximum Press)

Essential Business Tactics for the Net, Larry Chase with Nancy C. Hanger (1998, John Wiley & Sons)

Net Gain: Expanding Markets Through Virtual Communities, John Hagel III and Arthur G. Armstrong (1997, Harvard Business School Press)

Robert Colbert focuses on building and promoting your own website, another useful and economical promotion method that would not exist without the Internet.

Web Promotion Means More Sales

By Robert Colbert

The Internet continues to grow in importance. More people around the world are using it, and they're using it more often than ever. According to the Internet Advertising Bureau, more than 67.5 million U.S. computers were connected to the Internet in January 1999, a fifty percent increase from the previous year. This number is expected to rise with the number of computer-based companies and advertisers continuing to enter the market.

Web promotion is vital to making e-commerce, or Internet sales, an integral part of your company.

I have been involved with various facets of the Internet for more than five years. I graduated from Arizona State University with a Bachelor's degree in Journalism. During my time at ASU, my involvement with the Internet grew in large part because of my career focus. The course load required spending time on the World Wide Web, which increased my desire to learn more about the Internet. I currently work for an Arizona company that acts as a portal for both cyber-surfers and casual browsers alike. I am also involved with the site's search engine on a daily basis, inputting website submissions and updating our database with local Arizona sites.

Involving yourself with Web promotion can actually be a lot easier than you think. With the ever-increasing number of websites on the Internet, promotion on the Web is not as difficult as it was 10 years ago.

Amazon.com, Bluemountainarts.com and AOL Shopping are attracting record numbers of virtual visitors, and stores such as Wal-Mart are devoting more attention to Internet-based retail because of the growth. Even though you may not be reaching for Amazon-type traffic, the potential for substantial growth clearly makes Web promotion attractive to any business.

Simple, Direct Messages

The idea behind promoting yourself on the Internet is similar to that found in mainstream advertising and retail. Keep things simple and direct. Don't confuse the consumer with too many different messages, and above all be clear about what it is you want to promote. Whether it is a product or an idea, a direct approach is usually the best one. By incorporating a few simple steps, just about anyone should be able to promote a book, idea, or company on the World Wide Web.

Check Out the Cyber-Territory

One of the most important aspects of Web promotion is looking at what is already out there. Surf the Web as often as possible, looking at all the sites you come across. In order to be a successful promoter, you have to shop the competition the way a good consumer does. Find the things you do and don't like on other sites and write them down as a good list for you to refer to when putting together and promoting your own site.

Begin thinking about your reactions as an everyday consumer. What is it that drives you to a certain store in search of a particular item that can be found elsewhere? What is it about a commercial that draws you to a product—a familiar face, such as an actor or actress? Are you drawn to the logo or label? Or is it just that the product looks exciting or fun?

Take a look at the top sites on the Web, such as AOL shopping and Blue Mountain Arts. Remember to specifically shop the sites in the same category as your Web page for hints, as well. Take notes detailing why something was of particular interest to you. What was it about the graphics and layout that made you want to keep looking around? What turned you off about a page? Was it difficult to navigate? Was the information presented in a clear way? Would you go back to that site?

Ask people that you know the same questions. Get as much input as possible in order to get a general idea of dos and don'ts for sites. This will give you a better idea of what people, other than yourself, are looking to see on the Web.

Looks Are Important

The common thread for any repeat business, on the Web or otherwise, is appearance. Consumers want something nice to look at and easy to use. In handling Web promotion, appearance is probably the most important aspect for getting repeat visitors. There is an abundance of Web pages covering basically the same issues and events. Without any way to interpret a product's quality, consumers make their decisions on which site to visit primarily based on one thing: appearance.

Find a way to make your site stand out. Whether you add a little or a lot to your site, it's important for the page to contain something that makes viewers stop and take notice; otherwise they will click right past the page. If something is too bright, too loud, or just plain annoying, surfers will move on. The appearance of a site has to give a viewer the feeling of control. A Web designer generally should not create a page that is cluttered or looks unorganized. When designing your page, try to give it an individual quality that stands out from the others in the same category.

This allows people to distinguish your site as something original, different, or more informative. It also helps that people don't have to go searching all over the Web for information they can find at one place. You want a viewer to be enticed into staying because of the site's use of information[1] and graphics. Remember to try making your site appealing to others. Ask around after you've designed a page to see what people think.

By creating an attractive, distinct design through a combination of graphics, layout and/or text, your site can be the one everyone wants to see.

Keep Sites Organized

Be direct and to the point. Have you ever had a salesperson bombard you with information, even after you told them what you were looking for? Or have you ever gone into a store only to find it mashed together with so many items in an unorganized way that it made you want to leave? Web pages can have the same problem.

When searching on a Web page, viewers don't want to be burdened with trying to locate specific information if it's tucked away in the lower right-hand corner. Grouping links, graphics, and text in a coherent manner increases the chances of someone taking the time to thoroughly look at a site. Try not to spend too much time on fluff, such as blinking photos or dancing mice. It's not necessary on the Web, especially for promotion. In many cases, it can actually turn people off. Be succinct, yet enticing. Draw people in with clarity.

Spread the Word

After designing the site that's right for you, your next step in promotion should be spreading the word about your site. One of the best ways to accomplish this involves search engines. There are

---

[1] Please note that without good information (or content), your design won't keep surfers on the page either. Remember that many Web visitors are drawn in by search engines, which emphasize the content, not the design, of your page. With content being equal, a good design is crucial to repeat visits and your image as a professional. LFR

thousands of search engines on the Web today. Some of them only handle local sites, while others accept Web pages of various categories and locations on the Internet. It is important to have your website in as many search engines as possible because they provide maximum exposure to your audience. Use words that fully explain what is on your site when listing descriptions. People searching the Web view the descriptions as the headline for any website.

If your description is vague and boring, don't expect many visitors. Surfing the Web is like reading a newspaper; some articles are read thoroughly, while others are skipped, but the headlines are what draw readers in.

In a lot of cases, it is more time-consuming than anything else to have your site listed in hundreds of search engines. Start with free site submission areas on the bigger, more well-known sites, such as Netscape, Looksmart, Yahoo, and Lycos. But don't stop there. When you are on the Web, look for any links involving site submissions and click away.

If you're willing and able to spend a few extra dollars on promoting your site, few things could be easier than having your site listed on many engines. The Internet has an abundance of areas dedicated to placing Web pages in "hundreds of search engines," based on varying price scales. Make sure you know exactly where your site is submitted for the price you pay. After all, it doesn't do you any good to pay for submissions that don't happen. Although it's fun and easy to pay others to handle your site submissions, the job is far from over.

Sell, Sell, Sell

In order to make your website a permanent presence on the Internet, the last bit of promoting falls squarely on your shoulders. Sell, sell, and sell. When you send a message on e-mail, add the URL (Universal Resource Locator, or Web address) to your signature.

When you reply to a message, add the URL. If you are going to be promoting various sites at different times I suggest adding a little tease to your signature. For example, "Get the book you want at www.books4you.com" or "For the trip of a lifetime, travel to www.flyfast.com." That way people will begin looking for the new URL and will be excited to look at your latest promotion. Little things like that add up and can help turn a small site into a big one.

Link Up for Success

One partnership that you should seek out for Web promotion involves contacting other businesses on the Web to provide common links between the site. Many times, this will include building a separate page dedicated to links to various sites. For those promoting a specific product or a page that changes on a regular basis, using a link exchange can make your site the starting point for Web contact. This decision also helps drive traffic to your new site, and more importantly, to your latest promotion.

First Impressions Count

Promoting yourself or your business on the Web doesn't have to be costly or aggravating. It can be easy and efficient with great rewards. Getting people to notice your book, company, or even your resume encompasses the strategy practiced every day at malls, shops, and in television commercials.

The success of your promotion depends heavily upon the appearance of your site and spreading the knowledge of your site to others. The more people who know about your pages and their quality, the more likely they are to return. But if you only remember one thing about Web promotion, remember you never get a second chance to make a good, first impression.

Afterword

Promote Like a Pro started as an idea to share the wealth of information and knowledge I have gained through many years of producing and marketing books. When I started sharing my ideas, I soon realized that a lot of credit for those ideas belongs to those professionals who surround me on a daily or by-the-project basis. So this book gave me a chance to give credit where credit was due. As we were putting together the pieces of *Promote Like a Pro,* I realized that certain pieces of this puzzle were still missing. So I reached out to the community and sought experts who could fill some of those gaps in our promotional knowledge. Experts responded from places I never dreamed. Some found us, and others came highly recommended. Some even thought there might be someone who was a step ahead of them in their own area of expertise and generously referred these people to us. I have made some new friends along the way, added to my resources, and I hope I have given you a treasure chest of marketing advice. Those who contributed their chapters did so knowing I had to work within a budget. They did so to give to you what was at one time most likely given to them. They were generous in reaching out and helping others who might be getting started or who needed help keeping their wheels in motion.

I continue to fight the same battles of producing and marketing books on a budget. It is with respect and gratitude that I thank each person who graciously contributed their expertise to this book. I take my hat off to each of you. Many contributors not only worked within my budget, they worked within my time frame. "You want it when? And you are paying what?" Although not one person said that out loud, I'm sure that thought entered their minds—it did mine. My schedule often infringed upon theirs, but each of them still made time for *Promote Like a Pro.* If you like what they have to say, write them, e-mail them, or drop us a note. We will make sure your comments reach them.

One expert who was right here on the Five Star staff for many years is Mary Hawkins, who worked for me from almost the beginning as my sole editor. She not only edited a number of our books, but assisted in the development of many of our mailing lists. Her advice is invaluable. It was a surprise to learn that Mary was 80 years old when she first started working with Five Star, but it shouldn't have been. She had had a full career wearing more hats than I can mention here (journalist, editor, and for many years providing promotion and information services for two national educational associations, and more) before she joined up with us in 1989. She retired—or so she thinks—from Five Star in the past year, and I wanted to extend her special thanks, not only for her help here but for all her support through the years.

I also wanted to take this opportunity to thank other Five Star members who have helped us along the way. These folks include Paul M. Howey, who is a writer/editor extraordinaire and who never forgets the anniversary date of when he joined the Five Star family; Lynlie Hermann, whose artistic talents as a graphic designer can be enjoyed in many of our previous book covers, logo designs, and marketing materials; Kevin Dietz, who is our proofreader and catcher of mistakes; and Susan Grapentine, who has a brilliant mind for marketing and helped us name this book. Two other special people labor behind the scenes. Although they remain hidden from you, it's their work and efforts that make us shine. They are Chris Cook and Kim Scott. Chris has been our webmaster for several years. People from around the world continue to compliment our **www.FiveStarSupport.com** website, and it's Chris that we have to thank for that. Kim recently joined the Five Star family and adds her talents to our staff of dynamic graphic designers. Kim not only designed this book cover, but contributes her talents to our websites. Then, there is Suzi Prokell who has contributed to our publicity efforts. Suzi is a media pro, and we are grateful for all her efforts. I better not forget the person who acted as the assistant editor for *Promote Like a Pro* (and who is also my office manager), Sue DeFabis. Sue does her best to keep me on task. She proofreads and edits just about everything that crosses my desk, and recently helped me get through my class papers. (I'm not sure who was happier when I completed my Introduction to Mediation course, Sue or me!) She knows me all too well and stays with me in spite of it. Although other members of my staff have the ability and talent to take the concept of a book and bring it to life, Sue has the ability to polish my words, keep me in line, and make Five Star look better in the process.

Last, but most importantly, I want to thank Sal Caputo for helping to pull this all together. It's one thing to have an idea for a book, and it's another thing to be fortunate to have someone like Sal to make it real. His insights along the way helped to improve each chapter. He graciously worked with the contributing authors as we tried to work around their hectic schedules. What does that say about Sal's hectic schedule? He always made time to answer another e-mail, make that extra call, and edit just one more chapter. I kept promising that the most-recent chapter submitted was going to be the last chapter. What started out as a three-phase book, turned into a four- or five-, or was it a six-phase book? You'll have to ask Sal. He'll be able to tell you. Thanks, Sal, for turning my dream into reality!

It's All Up to You

Now that you've read *Promote Like a Pro*, you're ready to start on your promotional journey. If you are anything like me, you couldn't wait until you reached the end of this book before trying out our techniques.

I want to hear from you. I want to know what you tried, what worked, and what did not. We will be sharing ideas at **www.BookProducer.com**, adding new advice, answering specific questions, and presenting occasional new articles on different aspects of book promotion.

You don't have to go it alone. We don't want you to stop with *Promote Like a Pro*. We'd like you to use it as a starting point. *PLP* readers will be rewarded with new advice, access to media lists at reduced prices, and one month's free listing at **www.CheapPublicity.com** (this offer can be combined with any other promotional offers at the site itself).

CheapPublicity is the low-cost media connection, a site that is visited by journalists seeking expert sources, talk-show hosts looking for guests, and organizations recruiting guest speakers. List yourself there to tap into these opportunities.

We would also appreciate your feedback on the usefulness of this book, on any different aspects of promotion you'd like to see addressed in future editions, as well as any problems you encounter in the course of your promotional work.

You can send e-mail to **Radke@FiveStarSupport.com** or write to:

Five Star Publications, Inc.
P.O. Box 6698
Chandler, AZ 85246-6698
Attn: Book Producer

Now, it's your turn to Promote Like a Pro! Good luck!

Linda F. Radke
Chandler, Arizona
February 2000

Index

customers
building good will with, 63–69
developing a database of, 47–48, 52, 72, 171
finding best, 72–74
finding target audience, 31, 42, 44 72–74, 75–76

D

direct mail, 47–49
list of resources, 48
sending to friends and family, 64
target audience for, 48
tips for success, 49
distributors
discount taken by, 7
elements used to judge finished book, 4–5
library, 7
working with, 6–8
domain names, setting up on Internet, 158
donating copies of book, to generate goodwill, 67

E

e-zine (electronic newsletter), publishing, 46–47, 57, 164–165
Editor & Publisher, 96
editorial calendar, 56
editors
being persistent with, 104–105
book review, 108–109
sending follow-up note, 105
sending press kit to, 98–99, 102–103

working with, 56, 58, 97–105
800 number, having to increase sales, 151–152, 153
expectations about publicity, being realistic, 17–19

F–G

foreword of book, using well known name to write, 16–17
Fox, Larry (contributor)
biographical sketch, viii–ix
on promoting book on the Internet, 167–174
free publicity, 55–63
on radio & television programs, 118–131,133–134
public speaking, 55
schmoozing with media, 124
writing articles and columns, 55, 56–58, 73, 111–115
galley copies, using for advance publicity, 8, 9, 32
gift basket business, 63–65, 69–70
giveaways, using for promotion, 54, 143
good will, building with customers, 63–69

I

ideas
attention getting, 137
being open to new, 67–68
Internet. *See also* websites
advantages of, 156–157
attaching a signature when posting, 163–164, 179–180
domain names and, 158

public speaking
  amount spent on profes-
    sional speakers annually, 79
  for building visibility, 80
  for creating credibility, 79–80
  free publicity, using for, 55
  guidelines for, 58–60
  by invitation, 79
  as positive environment for
    success, 79
  providing differentiation from
    other speakers, 80–83
  using online forums for, 165
  using to create sales, 78–87
publicist
  acting as your own, 120–121
  finding an economical, 5–6
  hiring, 34, 126
publicity, 30–34. *See also* marketing; promotions
  advance, getting, 8–13
  aims of, 17–18
  challenges of, 14–16
  determining target audience
    for, 31, 42, 44, 72–74, 75–76
  getting free, 55–63, 73,
    111–115, 118–131, 133–134,
  having a plan, 2
  how different from
    advertising, 2
  keeping expectations
    realistic, 17–19
  misconception surrounding,
    30
  newspapers, using, 90–96
  television, using, 118–131
  tie-ins, 12–14
  timing of, 30
  unknown writers, and, 16–17
  working all the angles,
    15–16, 121

R

radio. *See also* talk radio;
  television
  advertising on, 41–43
  book sales through use of,
    142–143
  being interviewed on,
    136–137, 140–144
  finding right match, 134
  local news programs and,
    133–134
  needs of programmers,
    132–134, 139, 150
  sending contact information
    to, 135, 144
  tips for successful interview
    on, 142, 152–153
Radke, Linda (author/
  contributor)
  biographical sketch, v–vi
  on nuts and bolts of publish-
    ing, 2–24
relationship marketing, 50–53
  examples of, 51–52, 53
  guidelines for, 52–53
  review copies, using for
    marketing, 19, 102, 108,
    110
  reviewing sources. *See* book
    reviews

S

Sabah, Joe (contributor)
  biographical sketch, xi
  on using talk radio for
    promotion, 145–154
sales
  accepting credit cards,
    151–152

on getting free publicity on television, 118–131

trade shows and conferences, 54

Twelve Gifts of Birth, The (Costanzo), 65, 66

Ulrich's International Periodical Directory, 108

W

Wallace, Sarah Eden (contributor)
biographical sketch, xiii
on working with editors at media outlets, 97–105

websites. *See also* Internet
criteria for evaluating, 170
information to include on, 159–160
keeping organized, 178
linking to other sites, 161–162, 167, 170–173, 180
look of, importance of, 177–178, 180
promoting your own, 160, 179–180

providing free excerpts from your book, 167
researching other sites in subject area, 168
sample letter for permission to link to other, 172
search engines, using for marketing, 160–161, 168, 178–179
tips to make site productive, 158–159
using for book sales and promotion, 157–160, 175–180

Westheimer, Mary (contributor)
biographical sketch, xiii–xiv
on using the Internet to promote and sell books, 156–166

wholesalers. *See* distributors

Winfrey, Oprah, sending promotional information to, 76

wire services, using for publicity, 12

word-of-mouth publicity, 66

World Wide Web. *See* Internet, websites